Excel

ADVANCED SKILLS

ENGLISH

YEAR 3

AGES 8–9

# WRITING WORKBOOK

Get the Results You Want!

PASCAL PRESS

Laura Anderson

Reprinted 2017, 2018, 2020, 2021, 2022, 2024, 2026

ISBN 978 1 74125 403 7

Pascal Press
PO Box 250
Glebe NSW 2037
www.pascalpress.com.au

Publisher: Vivienne Joannou
Project editor: Rosemary Peers
Edited by Rosemary Peers
Series developer: Laura Anderson
Series consultant: Kristine Brown
Answers checked by Glenda Walsh
Cover and page design by DiZign Pty Ltd
Typeset by Kim Webber
Printed by Vivar Printing/Green Giant Press

# Contents

# To the student

*This book will help you with your writing tasks, in English and in other subjects.*

*There are eight units altogether, each focusing on a different type of text. Some texts are imaginative, such as narratives and poems. Others are factual, such as reports and explanations.*

*Each unit contains an introduction that explains the purpose of the text and its special features. There are also examples of students' first drafts. These are followed by practice exercises that aim to improve the draft. Some of the exercises focus on the structure of the text while others focus on its language features. There is one example of a student's final draft. Make sure you read it carefully and answer the questions beside each paragraph.*

*At the end of the unit is a text in which words, sentences or paragraphs are missing. You should try to fill in the missing sections, using the step-by-step improvement exercises to help you. In the final activity, you are given a list of topics and you have to choose one to write about.*

*Most of the activities can be written in this book, but you will have to use your own paper for the final writing activity. I suggest you buy a notebook or folder for this. If you are not sure how to write something, use the sample texts and the checklists to help you.*

*It is best to work through the book from Unit 1 to the end. This will help you build on skills you have already learnt. However, if you are learning about a particular type of text in school, you could do that unit in the book. For example, if you are learning about information reports, you could do Unit 6.*

*It is important that you have a dictionary and a thesaurus handy as you work through the book, and that you ask for help if you need it. There is also a word bank of useful vocabulary at the end of the book to help you with your writing.*

*I hope you enjoy reading the texts and doing the activities.*

*Good luck!*

*Laura Anderson*

# About this book

This book consists of eight units, each covering a different type of text. Each unit contains two samples of students' first drafts, followed by exercises designed to help the students improve their drafts. There is one example of a final draft, which models the text for students. Students are then asked to complete a partially constructed final draft, and finally to construct a text independently. These last two activities allow students to put the knowledge they have acquired into practice.

The units are organised as follows:

## An introduction to the type of text

This page looks at the features of the text. There are also short exercises to help students identify the type of text or its features.

## Student A: Writing the first draft

These two pages focus on the planning and writing of the first draft. There is a comprehensive checklist that enables students to identify the features that have or have not been included in the draft, as well as other short exercises.

## A step-by-step improvement plan

This section contains steps designed to help students improve the draft. Some of the steps focus on the structure of the text, while others focus on the language features.

## Writing the final draft

The final draft is an example of a more advanced student's writing. It is accompanied by comments that point out the features of the text, as well as questions that ask students to identify some of the features.

## Student B: Writing the first draft

The second half of the unit looks at another first draft, followed by a step-by-step improvement plan. Students are then asked to complete a partially constructed final draft.

## Your turn

The final page of the unit contains a list of topics, from which students choose one to write about. There is a checklist to guide students in their writing. There is also a note directing students to a word bank at the back of the book where they can find useful vocabulary to help them with the writing task.

## Word bank

At the end of the book is a word bank where students will find useful lists of words and phrases to help them complete their independent writing tasks.

# Unit 1 Writing a recount

## Looking at recounts

A **recount** tells about something that has already happened, in the order in which the events took place.

When you write a diary entry, a letter or email about something that happened to you, or a story about someone's life, you are writing a recount.

A **recount** should have:

- an **orientation**, or introduction, that tells your reader **who** was involved, **what** happened, and **when** and **where** it happened.
- a **sequence of events** in the order in which they took place.
- a **conclusion,** which can contain your **personal comment** about the events. For example: *At five o'clock it was time to go home.* **I really enjoyed the party!**

**1** Read this **recount** and then answer the questions.

Yesterday I went to my friend Ben's house to see his new puppy.

His puppy is really cute. We played with it for a bit and then we kicked a ball around in the backyard. We also played games on Ben's computer. We stopped when Ben's mum called us for lunch.

After lunch we finished our computer game and then it was time for me to go home. Ben and I had a great time!

**a** When did the events take place?

______________________

______________________

**b** Where did they happen? ______________________

**c** Who was involved? ______________________

**d** Find in the recount the **past tense** of the following verbs and underline them:

go   play   kick   stop   call   finish   is   have

**e** Underline in the recount the writer's **personal comment** about the events.

**2** Put a tick (✓) next to the events that have already happened.

**a** Tomorrow I am going to Melbourne. ☐

**b** Yesterday I got a new bicycle. ☐

**c** I am trying to do my homework! ☐

**d** We went to the zoo last week. ☐

**e** We visited Hong Kong last year. ☐

**f** I will visit my friend on the weekend. ☐

# Student A: Lily's draft

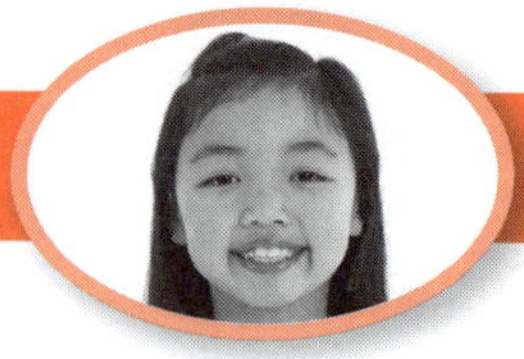

The students in Year 3 are putting together a booklet in which they each tell about a special event in their life.

Lily is going to write a **recount** about her eighth birthday party.

First she looked at some photos of her party to remind herself of the things that happened. Then she wrote a sentence for each photo.

1. Match the sentences with the photos by writing the correct letter in the box next to each photo.

**a** Jessica and Annie brought me presents.

**b** I blew out the candles.

**c** Annie gave me a book.

**d** Everybody sang 'Happy Birthday' to me.

2. Write the sentences from question 1 in the order in which it is most likely the events happened.

# Writing the first draft

This is Lily's **first draft**. Read what she wrote and then answer the questions.

## My Eighth Birthday Party

I turned eight in December. I had a party at my house. My friends came to my party.

Jessica and Annie came early. They brought me presents. Annie gave me a book. Jessica gave me an art set. I got lots of other presents.

Everybody sang 'Happy Birthday' to me. I blew out the candles.

We played games.

My friends went home.

1. A good **recount** should have the following features. Tick (✓) the ones that Lily has used.

   **a** an **orientation** (first paragraph) that tells **who**, **what**, **when** and **where** ☐

   **b** **events** told in the **order** in which they happened ☐

   **c** **time connectives** to **link** the **events** (e.g. *then* or *next*) ☐

   **d** **phrases** that tell **when**, **where** and **how** things were done (e.g. *at my house*) ☐

   **e** **verbs** written in the **past tense** (e.g. *turned* or *had*) ☐

   **f** **correct spelling** and **punctuation** ☐

   **g** a **conclusion** (last paragraph) that includes the writer's own **opinion** or **thoughts** about the events in the recount ☐

2. Lily has used two phrases that tell **when** and **where** in her draft.

   Underline the phrase that tells:

   **a** when she turned eight.

   **b** where she had a party.

3. Lily has also remembered to write in the past tense.

   Find the **past tense** of these verbs in the draft and underline them:

   **a** bring **b** get **c** sing **d** blow **e** go

4. Find three more **past-tense verbs** in Lily's draft and write them in the boxes.

   **a** ☐ **b** ☐ **c** ☐

# Step-by-step improvement plan

Lily wants to make her **recount** more interesting. First she'll do these practice exercises. Can you help her complete them?

## Step 1: Add detail with phrases

**Phrases** are groups of words. They add detail to your sentences by telling **when**, **where** and **how** things are done.

For example: *I had a party* **at my house**.

1. Underline the **phrases** that tell **when**, **where** or **how** in the following sentences.
   - **a** My party was supposed to start at 2.30 pm.
   - **b** I heard a knock at the door.
   - **c** I opened Annie and Jessica's presents straight away.
   - **d** We all gathered around the table to sing 'Happy Birthday'.
   - **e** I blew out the candles with a single breath!
   - **f** Afterwards we played games in the garden.
   - **g** The party ended at five o'clock.

2. Now write the **phrases** you underlined in numbers 1e, f and g under the correct headings.

| | |
|---|---|
| **When** | |
| **Where** | |
| **How** | |

## Step 2: Link events with time connectives

**Time connectives** are **words** and **phrases** that show the **order** in which things happened.

For example: **First** *everyone sang 'Happy Birthday'.* **Then** *I blew out the candles.*

Complete the sentences below with a **time connective** from the box. You have been given the first letter of the word or phrase to help you. Use each time connective once.

| | | | | | |
|---|---|---|---|---|---|
| meanwhile | at last | finally | then | after that | afterwards |

1. I waited and waited for my friends to arrive. A_______________ I heard a knock at the door. It was Annie and Jessica.
2. A_______________ my other friends started to arrive. We put the presents on a table. There were so many of them!
3. M_______________, Mum was getting everything ready in the dining room. She and Grandma had decorated the room with balloons and streamers. It looked fantastic!
4. We ate the delicious food that Mum had set out and t________ it was time to bring out the birthday cake!
5. A_______________ we played games in the garden. We had so much fun!
6. F_______________ it was time for my friends to go home. I wouldn't have another birthday party for a whole year!

## Step 3: End with a good conclusion

The **conclusion** is the last paragraph. It should tell **how** the **events** in your recount **ended**. It should also include your **opinion** or **thoughts** about the events.

1. Here are three **conclusions** for Lily's recount. Tick (✓) the box next to the one that tells what Lily thought about her party.

A. My friends' parents came to collect them at five o'clock. I waved goodbye to them. ☐

B. My friends' parents came to collect them at five o'clock. They all thanked me for inviting them to my party and I thanked them for the lovely presents. That was definitely the best birthday party I've ever had! ☐

C. Most of my friends left at five o'clock. Jessica and Annie's parents came a bit later. We looked through my presents while we waited for them. Jessica's parents came first and Annie's parents came just after that. ☐

2. Add another sentence that tells what Lily thought about her presents.

When everyone had gone, I opened my presents. _______________________________

_______________________________________________

_______________________________________________

# Writing the final draft

This is Lily's **final draft**. It is now more interesting to read, don't you agree?

Read the comments about her **recount** on the left, and do the tasks on the right.

## Comments

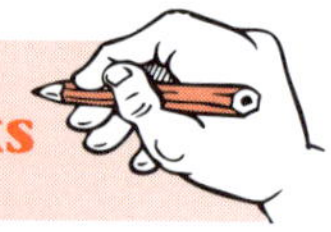

## Tasks

### My Birthday Party

*A clear* **orientation** *tells the reader* **who**, **what**, **when** *and* **where**.

I turned eight in December. Mum said I could have a big party at our house. She said I could invite my schoolfriends.

**1. Underline** the **phrase** that tells **where**.

*Using* **time connectives** *links events and makes the writing flow.*

My party was supposed to start at 2.30 pm. I couldn't wait for my friends to arrive! At last I heard a knock at the door. It was Annie and Jessica. They were early, so I opened their presents straight away. Annie gave me a colourful picture book and Jessica gave me an art set.

**2. Circle** the **past tense** of *is*, *cannot* and *give*.

After that my other friends started to arrive. I put their presents on the table so I could open them later. There were so many of them!

**3. Highlight** the **time connective**.

*Using* **phrases** *that tell* **when**, **where** *and* **how** *adds detail to sentences.*

Meanwhile, Mum was getting everything ready in the dining room. She and Grandma had decorated the room with balloons and streamers. It looked fantastic! We ate the delicious food that Mum had prepared and then it was time to bring out the birthday cake. Grandma had baked it and it was beautiful. I blew out all eight candles with a single breath!

**4. Underline** the **phrases** that tell **how**:

a the room had been decorated.

b Lily blew out the candles.

Afterwards we played our favourite games in the garden. We had so much fun!

**5. Circle** the **time connective**.

*Adding a* **personal comment** *helps round off the recount.*

Finally my friends' parents came to collect them. They all thanked me for inviting them to my party and I thanked them for the lovely presents. That was definitely the best birthday party I've ever had!

**6. Highlight** the writer's personal **opinion** about the party.

# Student B: Zac's draft

Zac, another Year 3 student, really enjoyed the class's excursion to the zoo, so he is going to write about it for the Year 3 booklet.

These were some of the photos he took that day.

1. Zac wrote these phrases on the backs of the photos. Match the **phrases** with the photographs by writing the correct letter in the box next to each photo.

   **a** watching the seal show
   **b** eating lunch
   **c** at the bird show
   **d** laughing at the chimps

2. Now expand the phrases to make **sentences**.

   For example: *We had a great time* **watching the seal show**.

**a** ______________________________

______________________________

**b** ______________________________

______________________________

**c** ______________________________

______________________________

**d** ______________________________

______________________________

# Writing the first draft

This is Zac's **first draft**. Read it and then answer the questions.

### Our Visit to the Zoo

In February our class visited the zoo.

We went on a bus. Our teachers divided us into groups. I was with Mrs Gonzalez.

Mrs Gonzalez took us to see the chimps. We laughed at them. We went to see the giraffes, the reptiles and the rainforest. It was time for lunch. We watched the bird show and listened to a talk. We watched the seal show.

We got on the bus to come back to school. I really enjoyed seeing all the animals!

1. Tick (✓) the correct answers. Which of these things has Zac remembered to include in his draft?
   - a an interesting **orientation** that tells **who**, **what**, **when** and **where** ☐
   - b **events** in the **order** in which they happened ☐
   - c **time connectives** to **link events** and make the **writing flow** ☐
   - d **phrases** that tell **when**, **where** and **how** things were done ☐
   - e **past-tense verbs** ☐
   - f **correct spelling** and **punctuation** ☐
   - g a **personal comment** in the **conclusion** ☐
2. Like Lily, Zac has also remembered to write in the past tense.

   Find the **past tense** of these verbs in the draft and underline them:

   a go    b is    c laugh
3. Zac has remembered to include a **personal opinion** in his conclusion. Find and underline it.

# Step-by-step improvement plan

Zac also wants to make his **recount** more interesting. He will start by doing some practice exercises. Help him complete them.

## Step 1: Start with a good orientation

The **orientation** is the opening paragraph. It should:
- **capture** your **reader's attention** and make him or her want to read on.
- give a clear picture of **who** and **what** the recount is about, and **when** and **where** the events took place.

Which of these opening **paragraphs** would be a better way for Zac to start his recount?

A When we got back to school this year, Mrs Gonzalez gave us the exciting news—we were going on an excursion to the zoo to learn more about endangered animals. ☐

B At the beginning of February Mrs Gonzalez said we were going to the zoo. She gave us a note that our parents had to sign. The note told us what to bring to the zoo. ☐

C In February we went to the zoo. A bus took us there and brought us back to school. This is what we saw and did at the zoo. ☐

## Step 2: Add detail with phrases

Zac has written these phrases to give more information about **when**, **where** and **how** things were done.

- from the shop
- around the enclosure
- under a shady tree
- at the zoo
- at feeding time
- by bus
- above my head
- with a treat

Use the **phrases** to add detail to these sentences. Use each phrase once.

For example: *We travelled to the zoo* **by bus**.

1. We saw lots of interesting animals ______________________________.
2. Three small chimpanzees were chasing each other ______________________________.
3. We got to the giraffes' enclosure ______________________________.
4. One of the birds hovered ______________________________.
5. I bought a souvenir ______________________________.
6. We found a good spot ______________________ to sit and have our lunch.
7. The trainer rewarded the seal ______________________________.

## Step 3: Link events with time connectives

Look at the map to find the **order** in which Zac did things at the zoo.

Use the **time connectives** in the box to link the events. Use each time connective once.

**Hint!** You have been given the first letter of two of the words to help you sequence the events correctly.

| | | | | | | |
|---|---|---|---|---|---|---|
| Before | Next | Last of all | After lunch | First | Then | Afterwards |

1. F________________ we went to see the chimps.
2. ________________ we made our way to the giraffes' enclosure.
3. A________________ Mrs Gonzalez took us to see the reptiles and the rainforest.
4. ________________ the bird show started, there was just enough time to have lunch.
5. ________________ we watched the bird show.
6. ________________ we listened to a talk on endangered animals.
7. ________________ we went to the seal show.

# Writing the final draft

Zac has started writing the **final draft** of his **recount**. Help him complete it by filling in the missing sections and then look in the answers section to compare what you have written with what Zac wrote.

**Hint!** Look at the map for ideas.

## Our Visit to the Zoo

Just after we got back to school this year, Mrs Gonzalez gave us the exciting news—we were going on an excursion to the zoo to learn more about endangered animals.

We travelled to the zoo by bus. When we arrived there, we were divided into groups. I was in Mrs Gonzalez's group.

First we went to see the chimps. Three small chimpanzees were chasing each other around the enclosure. They were so funny!

Afterwards we made our way to the giraffes' enclosure. **(Tell what happened at the giraffes' enclosure.)**

..............................................................................................................

..............................................................................................................

..............................................................................................................

..............................................................................................................

Next, Mrs Gonzalez took us to see the reptiles and the rainforest. I thought that some of the reptiles looked scary, especially the enormous grey crocodile, but the rainforest was cool and relaxing and I enjoyed looking at the colourful birds.

Before the bird show started, **(Tell where you had lunch.)**

..............................................................................................................

..............................................................................................................

..............................................................................................................

..............................................................................................................

After lunch we went to the bird show. It was brilliant! I couldn't believe how clever those birds were! One of them hovered right above my head. I thought it was going to use me as a perch!

Then we listened to a talk on endangered animals. It was very interesting, and we even got to hold a couple of the rainforest animals. It was the first time I'd ever touched a snake. I thought it would feel slimy, but its skin was dry.

**(Fill in a time connective.)** ........................................................ we watched the seal show. The seals performed some amazing tricks and their trainer rewarded them with a treat.

I was exhausted when we finally got onto the bus to come back to school, but I'd had a great time looking at all the animals.

# Your turn

Write a **recount** of about one page on one of the following. Use your own paper for this activity.

**Writing Checklist** Make sure your recount includes: ✓

- an **orientation** that tells who, what, when and where. ☐
- a **series of events**, told in the order in which they happened. ☐
- **phrases** that tell when, where and how things were done. ☐
- **time connectives** to link events. ☐
- **past-tense verbs**. ☐
- a **conclusion** that contains a **personal opinion** about the events in the recount. ☐

**Tip** Use **Lily's final draft** on page 6 and **Zac's final draft** on page 11 to help you write your recount.

Go to WORD BANK page 105 for useful vocabulary

1. Write about something you have experienced that was special in some way, such as a birthday party, a day at a fun park or a day at the beach.

   To help you, look back at how Lily wrote her recount.

2. Write about a class excursion that you found particularly interesting or that you really enjoyed.

   To help you, look at how Zac wrote his recount.

3. Write a recount that starts like this:

   *Everything went wrong for me yesterday—from the moment I got up in the morning until the moment I went to bed at night. It all started when I couldn't find my school shoes …*

   Continue the recount, telling about the things that went wrong for you yesterday.

4. Imagine you are a boy or girl in one of these photos. Write a recount based on the photo of your choice.

# Unit 2 Writing a procedure

## Looking at procedures

A **procedure** gives instructions on **how** to **make** or **do** something.

When you write out a recipe or an instruction to help someone play a game, you are writing a procedure.

A **procedure** should have:

- an **introduction** that tells your reader what you are going to make or do.
- a **list** of the ingredients or equipment you will need.
- a **series of steps** or instructions, given in the correct order.

**Hint!** We often use photographs, drawings or diagrams to help the readers understand the instructions.

Read the following **procedure** and then answer the questions.

This is how you make a paper aeroplane.

What you need: a sheet of A4 paper

Steps:

First, fold the paper in half lengthwise.

Next, fold the top two corners into the centre.

Then fold in the two long edges so that they meet on the centre fold.

After that, fold the centre line to hide all the other folds.

Finally, fold down the two top flaps to make the wings.

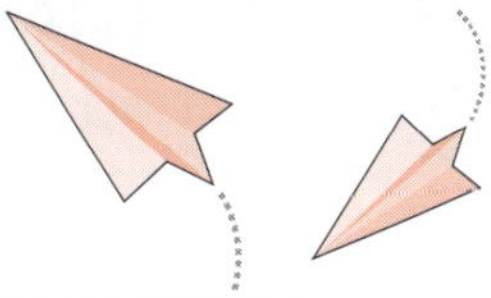

1. Underline the **sentence** that tells what the aim of the procedure is.
2. What **materials** are needed to make a paper aeroplane? ______________________
3. Circle the words that show the **order** in which the steps should be done.
4. Which is the **action verb** near the beginning of each sentence? ________________

# Student A: Navin's draft

Navin's Year 3 class is learning about healthy and unhealthy foods.
Every student has to think of some healthy ingredients to put on a sandwich.
Then they each have to write a **procedure** that explains how to make the sandwich.

First, Navin thought of all the things he would need.

## Ingredients

## Equipment

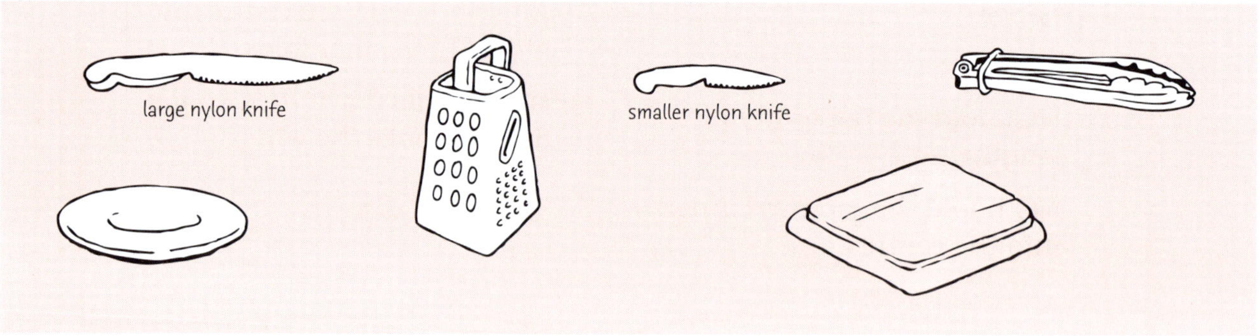


Write these words next to the pictures that don't have labels.

| | | | | |
|---|---|---|---|---|
| tomato | carrot | bread | lettuce leaves | cucumber |
| grater | tongs | chopping board | plate | |

# Writing the first draft

This is Navin's **first draft**. Read what he wrote and then answer the questions.

**Ingredients:**
wholemeal bread butter cooked chicken tomato cucumber lettuce leaves sprouts carrot beetroot mayonnaise

**Equipment:**
chopping board large nylon knife small nylon knife tongs grater small plate

**Steps:**
This is how to make the sandwich. Cut two slices of bread and spread some butter on them. Get shreds of chicken. Cut the tomato and cucumber into slices. Then I grated the carrot. I put the chicken, tomato, cucumber, sprouts, carrot, a slice of beetroot and some lettuce leaves on one slice of bread. I put a little bit of mayonnaise over the lettuce leaves. I covered everything with the other slice of bread. I cut the sandwich into two triangles and I served it on a plate.

1. A good **procedure** should contain the following features. Tick (✓) the ones that Navin has used.
   - a an **introduction** that tells what the **aim** of the procedure is ☐
   - b a **list** of the **ingredients** or equipment that you will need ☐
   - c a clear **series of steps**, or **instructions**, written in the **correct order** ☐
   - d **sentences** that **start** with an **action verb** for every step of the instructions (e.g. **Cut** *two slices of bread* or **Shred** *the chicken*) ☐
   - e **connectives** that show the **order** in which the actions are done (e.g. *first* or *after that*. (Sometimes the steps are numbered instead.) ☐
   - f **present-tense verbs** throughout (e.g. *make* or *grate*) ☐
   - g **correct spelling** and **punctuation** ☐
2. One important thing that Navin has forgotten is to use **commas** to separate the items in his list of ingredients and equipment. Fill them in for him.
3. Underline the sentences that start with **action verbs**.
4. Write the **phrases** that tell:
   - a where to put the mayonnaise. ______________________________
   - b how to cut the sandwich. ______________________________

# Step-by-step improvement plan

Navin is going to do some practice exercises to find ways to improve his **procedure**. Help him complete them.

## Step 1: Start with a clear introduction

The **introduction** is the first sentence or two of the procedure. It should tell your reader exactly what the **aim** of your procedure is.

1. Which would be the best **title** for Navin's procedure?

- How to Prepare a Healthy Snack ☐
- How to Choose Healthy Foods ☐
- How to Make a Chicken Salad Sandwich ☐

2. Which would be the best way for Navin to **start** his procedure?

- This is a healthy snack. ☐
- This is what you need to make a chicken salad sandwich. ☐
- Some snacks are unhealthy, but this one isn't. ☐

## Step 2: Start sentences with action verbs

**Action verbs** tell us **what** to do (e.g. *cut, spread* and *slice*). Starting a sentence with an action verb helps your reader focus on what he or she has to do.

Change these sentences so that they start with the **verb**. Make sure the verb is in the present tense, e.g. slice.

1. I grated the carrot. ______________________________

______________________________

2. I put the chicken on the bread. ______________________________

______________________________

3. I put mayonnaise over the lettuce leaves. ______________________________

______________________________

4. I covered it with the other slice. ______________________________

______________________________

5. I served it on a plate. ______________________________

______________________________

## Step 3: Use connectives to show order

**Connectives** show the **order** of actions (e.g. *first, next* or *then).*
They help us make sense of the instructions.

Connectives should come before the action verb at the beginning of the sentence.
For example: **First**, *cut two slices of bread.*

Arrange the following sentences so that the **order** is clear. Match the letters to the steps in the boxes below.

**Hint!** Use Navin's draft to help you.

**a** After that, slice the tomato and cucumber and grate the carrot.

**b** Next, use the large knife to cut two slices of bread from a wholemeal loaf. Spread butter on each slice.

**c** First, gather all your ingredients and equipment.

**d** Finally, layer all the ingredients on one slice of bread.

**e** Then, pull shreds off the chicken.

| Step 1 | Step 2 | Step 3 | Step 4 | Step 5 |
|---|---|---|---|---|
| | | | | |

## Step 4: Use verbs that give precise instructions

**Verbs** can tell us what **action** is happening and when it happens.
For example: **Slice** *the bread.*

Using precise verbs when giving instructions helps your reader perform the task correctly.
For example: *fry* is a more precise verb than *cook*.

Choose the more precise **verb** from the brackets to complete each sentence.

1. (Take, Pull) ______________ shreds from the chicken.
2. (Squirt, Place) ______________ mayonnaise on the lettuce leaves.

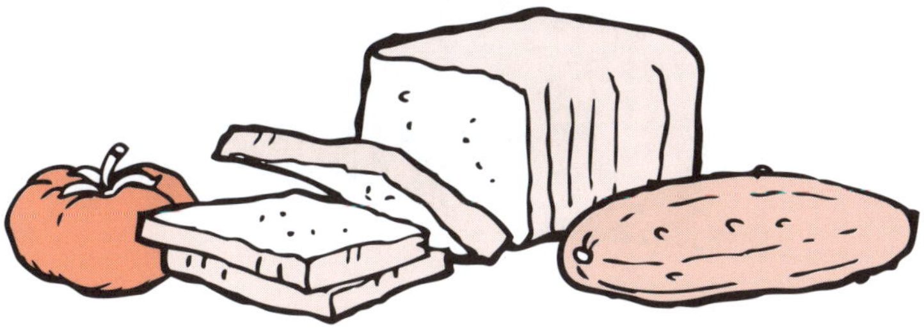

# Writing the final draft

This is Navin's **final draft**. Read the comments about his **procedure** on the left, and do the tasks on the right.

**Comments**

*Starting with an **introduction** lets the reader know what the aim of the procedure is.*

*Giving a **list** of ingredients and equipment helps the reader get organised.*

*Using **headings** and **paragraphs** makes the procedure easier to understand.*

*Using **connectives** shows the order in which the actions should be done.*

## How to Make a Chicken Salad Sandwich

This is what you need to make a chicken salad sandwich.

**Ingredients**: wholemeal bread, butter, cooked chicken, tomato, cucumber, lettuce leaves, sprouts, carrot, beetroot, mayonnaise

**Utensils**: large nylon knife, small nylon knife, tongs, grater, small plate

**Steps**:

First, cut two slices from a wholemeal loaf. Spread butter on each slice.

Next, pull shreds from the chicken and grate the carrot. Slice the tomato and cucumber.

Then place the chicken on one slice of bread. Add the tomato, cucumber, sprouts and carrot.

Use the tongs to place a slice of beetroot on the sandwich.

After that, place the lettuce leaves on the beetroot and squirt on some mayonnaise. Cover it with the other slice.

Finally, cut the sandwich into triangles and serve on a plate.

**Tasks**

1. **Underline** the **commas**.
2. **Circle** the **words** that describe the knives.
3. **Highlight** the **connective**.
4. **Circle** the **action verbs**.
5. **Highlight** the list of salad **ingredients**.
6. **Underline** the **verb** that means the same as *put*.
7. **Circle** the **connective**.
8. **Highlight** the **action verbs**.

# Student B: Lauren's draft

Lauren is in a different Year 3 class. Her class has also been learning about healthy and unhealthy foods. The students have to each write a **procedure** for making a healthy fruit salad.

Like Navin, Lauren starts by thinking about the ingredients she will need.

1 Use the **words** from the box to label the pictures.

| | | | | | | | |
|---|---|---|---|---|---|---|---|
| pineapple | mango | watermelon | banana | lemon | rockmelon | apple | papaya |

Then Lauren pictured all the utensils she would need.

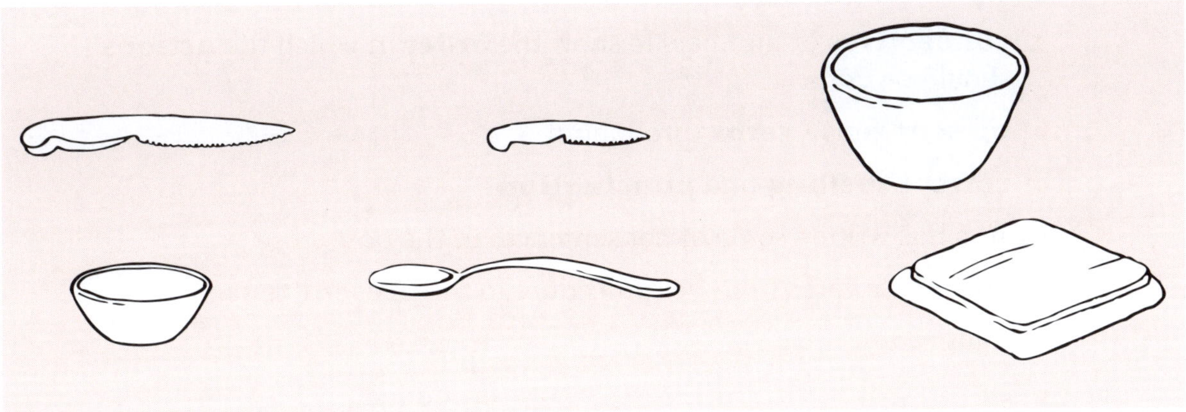

2 Now use these **words** to label the pictures.

| | | | |
|---|---|---|---|
| small bowl | chopping board | large nylon knife | large spoon |
| small nylon knife | large bowl | | |

# Writing the first draft

This is Lauren's **first draft**. Read it and then answer the questions.

## Eating Healthy Foods

**Ingredients:**
watermelon, papaya, rockmelon, pineapple, apple, banana, mango, lemon

**Utensils:**
chopping board, large nylon knife, small nylon knife, large bowl, small bowl, large spoon

**Steps:**
Peel the banana and chop up the apple. Put them in the big bowl. I squeezed some lemon juice over them. If you don't do this, the apples and bananas will turn brown. I cut up the watermelon, rockmelon, pineapple, papaya and mango. I added it to the bowl. I mixed everything together. I dished some of my healthy fruit salad into a small bowl.

1 Which of these features has Lauren remembered to include in her draft? Tick (✓) the correct answers.

a a clear **introduction** that tells the reader what the **aim** of the procedure is ☐

b a **list** of the **ingredients** and **utensils** needed ☐

c the **steps** or instructions for the procedure in the **correct order** ☐

d **sentences** that **start** with **action verbs** ☐

e **connectives** or numbers to show the **order** in which the **actions** should be done ☐

f **present-tense verbs** throughout ☐

g **correct spelling** and **punctuation** ☐

2 Lauren has written some of her sentences in the past tense.

Change these verbs from her procedure to the **present tense**.

a squeezed ____________ b asked ____________

c cut ____________ d added ____________

e mixed ____________ f dished ____________

3 Write the **adjectives** that Lauren has used to describe:

a thebowls. ____________

b the fruit salad. ____________

# Step-by-step improvement plan

Lauren is also going to do some practice exercises to find ways to improve her **procedure**. Help her complete them.

## Step 1: Start with a clear introduction

1. Lauren has called her procedure *Eating Healthy Foods.*

   What would be a better **title**?

   ______________________________

   ______________________________

2. Complete this sentence to show what the **aim** of Lauren's procedure is.

   This is how ______________________________

   ______________________________

## Step 2: Start sentences with action verbs

Write the **instruction** that should go with each of the following pictures. Remember to start each sentence with an **action verb**. The first one has been done for you.

Peel the banana.

______________________________

______________________________

______________________________

## Step 3: Use connectives to show order

Start each of these sentences with a **connective** to show that the actions are done one after the other. Find the connectives in the box.

**Hint!** Start with *First*.

| | | | | |
|---|---|---|---|---|
| after that | finally | first | then | next |

1. ________________, peel and slice the banana and put it in the large bowl. Use the small knife to do this.
2. ____________, wash and chop the apple and add it to the banana.
3. ____________________, squeeze the lemon juice over the apple and banana to stop them turning brown.
4. ____________, cut the rest of the fruit into chunks and add them to the bowl.
5. _________________, mix the fruit together with a large spoon.

## Step 4: Add interest and information with adjectives

**Adjectives** give information about nouns and pronouns.
For example: *a* **firm** *mango.*

Using adjectives to describe food can make it sound more appealing. Adjectives can also give more precise information about the food.

Complete the phrases below with adjectives from the box. Use each adjective once.

| | | | |
|---|---|---|---|
| seedless | juicy | ripe | crunchy |

1. a _________________ banana
2. a _________________ apple
3. a _________________ watermelon
4. _________________ strawberries

## Writing the final draft

Lauren has started writing the **final draft** of her **procedure**. Help her complete it, and then look in the answers section to compare what you have written with what Lauren wrote.

**Hint!** Look at Lauren's notes and the practice exercises for ideas.

### How to Make a Fruit Salad

**Opening statement:**

..........

..........

..........

**Ingredients:** watermelon, papaya, rockmelon, pineapple, apple, banana, mango, lemon

**Utensils:** chopping board, large nylon knife, small nylon knife, large bowl, small bowl, large spoon

**Steps:**

..........

..........

..........

..........

..........

..........

..........

..........

..........

..........

..........

..........

..........

..........

..........

## Your turn

Write a **procedure** of about one page on one of the following. Use your own paper for this activity.

**Writing Checklist** Make sure your procedure includes: ✓

- an **opening statement** that tells what the **aim** or **purpose** of the procedure is. ☐
- a **list** of the **ingredients** or **materials** that will be needed. ☐
- a clear **set of steps**, or instructions, given in the **correct order**. ☐
- **sentences** that **start** with **action verbs**. ☐
- **connectives** or numbers to show the **order** in which the **actions** should be done. ☐
- **present-tense verbs**. ☐
- **correct spelling** and **punctuation**. ☐

**Tip** Use **Navin's final draft** on page 18 and **Lauren's final draft** on page 23 to help you write your procedure.

Go to WORD BANK page 105 for useful vocabulary

1. Write a procedure that tells how to make a healthy tuna, cheese or egg sandwich.

   Use Navin's procedure as a model.

2. Write a procedure that tells how to make a healthy salad that includes at least five vegetables. Use Lauren's procedure as a model.

3. Write the procedure that students at your school have to follow from the time they arrive at school until the start of the first lesson. You could start like this:

   *First, go straight to your classroom and hang your bag on your hook.*

   Make your procedure into a poster.

# Unit 3 Describing a person

## Looking at descriptions

A **description** gives your reader a clear **picture** of a **person**, **place** or **thing**.

It is usually part of another text. In a narrative, it **helps tell your story**.

Sometimes a description can be a text on its own. In this case, it should have:

- an interesting **introduction** that gets your reader's attention and tells **what** your description is about.
- **paragraphs** that **describe** the person, place or thing.
- a **conclusion** that includes your **final comment** or **thought** about the person, place or thing.

**Descriptions** of people, places or things can be found in almost every type of text.

1. Where are you more likely to find these **descriptions**? Tick (✓) the correct answer.

**a**

Humpty Dumpty was a tubby little man who often sat on the high wall around the palace grounds.

information report ☐

narrative ☐

**b**

The kookaburra has a dark-brown eye-stripe through the face.

information report ☐

narrative ☐

2. Which sentence in each pair gives the clearer **description** of the person or place? Tick (✓) the correct answer.

**a**

The man arrived in a car. ☐

The tall man arrived in a silver car. ☐

**b**

The sun shone brightly on the still water. ☐

The sun shone on the water. ☐

# Student A: Nina's draft

Each student in Nina's Year 3 class has to describe the appearance and personal qualities of a person he or she knows well. Nina is going to write a **description** of her grandmother.

She starts by drawing a picture of her grandmother. Then she writes words and phrases to describe her grandmother around the picture.

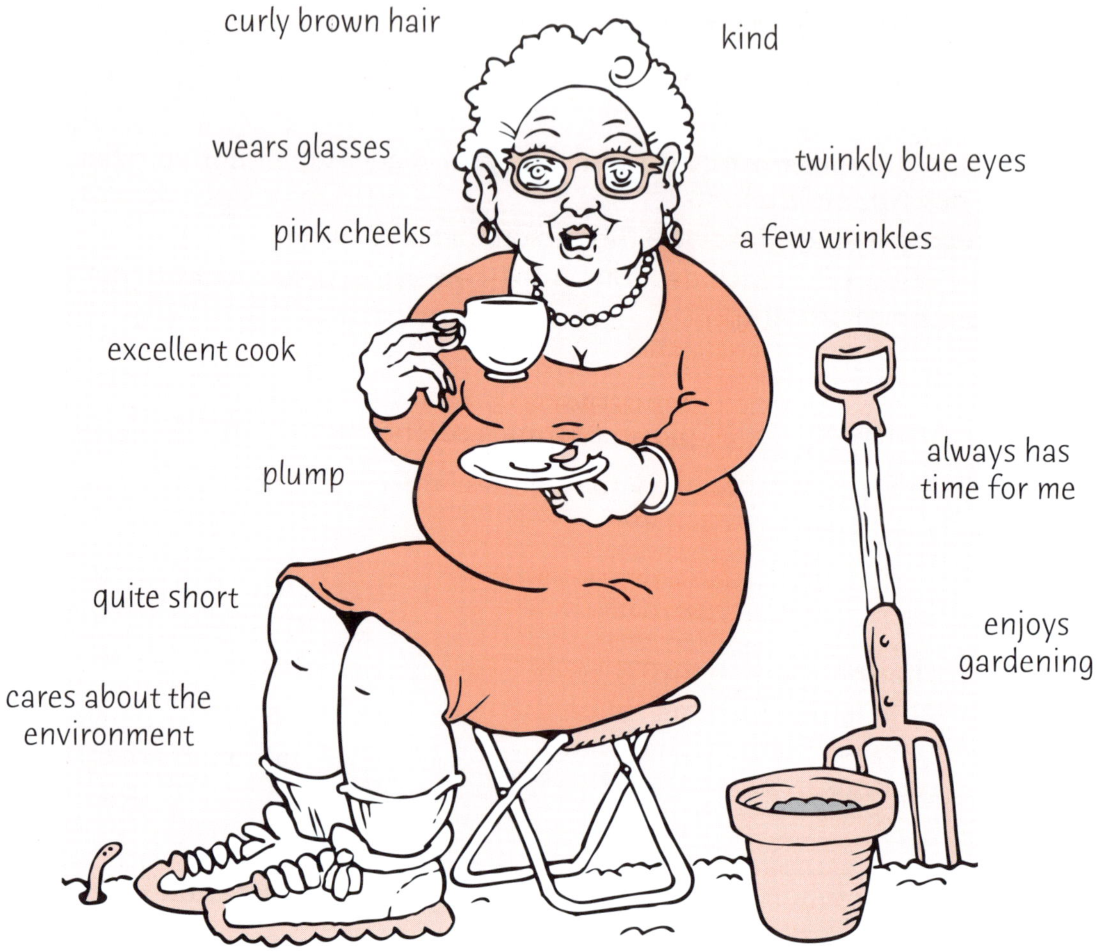


Nina has used a number of adjectives to describe her grandmother. Remember: adjectives add meaning to nouns.

1. List five **adjectives** that Nina has used.

______________________________

______________________________

2. Which two things could be described as her grandmother's hobbies?

______________________________

______________________________

# Writing the first draft

This is Nina's **first draft**. Read what she wrote and then answer the questions.

## My Grandmother

My grandmother has curly brown hair. She has twinkly blue eyes. She wears glasses. She has a few wrinkles on her face. She has pink cheeks. She is quite short. She is a bit plump. She enjoys gardening. She cares about the environment. She always has time for me. She is an excellent cook. She is kind.

1. A good **description** should contain the following features. Tick (✓) the ones that Nina has used.
   - a an interesting **introduction** to get her **reader's attention** ☐
   - b **paragraphs** that **describe** her grandmother ☐
   - c **adjectives** that **describe** her grandmother (e.g. *curly, blue* or *few*) ☐
   - d **present-tense verbs** (e.g. *has* or *wears*) ☐
   - e **conjunctions** to **link** ideas and make her writing flow (e.g. *but* or *because*) ☐
   - f **correct spelling** and **punctuation** ☐
   - g a **conclusion** that includes her final **comment** or **thought** about her grandmother ☐

2. Nina has remembered to use **present-tense verbs** throughout her description.

   Underline the present-tense verbs in these sentences from the draft.
   - a She has a few wrinkles on her face.
   - b She is quite short.
   - c She enjoys gardening.

3. Which **adjectives** could Nina use to describe her grandmother's food? Tick (✓) the ones that Nina could use.

| | | |
|---|---|---|
| delicious ☐ | clumsy ☐ | tasty ☐ |
| scrumptious ☐ | clever ☐ | heavenly ☐ |

# Step-by-step improvement plan

Help Nina improve her **description** by completing these practice exercises.

## Step 1: Start with an interesting introduction

The **introduction** is the opening paragraph. It should **grab** your **reader's attention** and make him or her want to carry on reading the rest of your description.

Use these **phrases** to complete the paragraph below.

fights to save the environment

call my grandmother Gran

sound fierce

very sweet and kind

I ______________________________.

She calls herself an eco warrior. That means she ______________________________

______________________________ It makes her

______________________________ but she's really ______________________________

______________________________.

## Step 2: Link ideas with conjunctions

**Conjunctions** are words like *and, but* and *so*. They **link**:

- **words** and **phrases** in sentences.
- two or more **clauses** or **sentences** to make one sentence.

Conjunctions make our writing **flow**. They also let us add **detail** to sentences.

Complete each of the following sentences with a **conjunction** from the box. Use each conjunction once only.

| | | | | | |
|---|---|---|---|---|---|
| and | but | or | so | yet | because |
| unless | until | when | while | although | |

1. My grandmother has curly brown hair ______________ twinkly blue eyes.
2. She is retired, ______________ she has lots of time to spend in the garden.

3. I enjoy visiting my grandmother ________________ she always has time for me.
4. My grandmother has a few wrinkles ______________ she does not look very old.
5. You can usually find her in the kitchen ___________________ out in the garden.
6. She lets me water the plants ___________ she does other jobs around the garden.
7. I visit her every weekend, _____________ she is busy with her conservation work.

## Step 3: End with a good conclusion

The **conclusion** is the last paragraph. It should contain a final **comment** about the person, place or thing you have described.

This is what Nina has written so far for her conclusion:

I always have a good time when I visit my grandmother because we do so many interesting things together.

Use the **phrases** below to help you write two more sentences to add to Nina's conclusion.

admire her because

one of my favourite

_______________________________________________

_______________________________________________

_______________________________________________

_______________________________________________

_______________________________________________

_______________________________________________

_______________________________________________

# Writing the final draft

This is Nina's **final draft**. Read the comments about her **description** on the left, and do the tasks on the right.

## Comments

*An interesting* **introduction** *captures the reader's attention.*

*Using* **interesting adjectives** *makes your description clearer.*

*Using* **conjunctions** *makes the writing flow.*

*The* **conclusion** *wraps up the description with a final comment about Gran.*

## My Grandmother

I call my grandmother Gran. She calls herself an eco warrior. That means she fights to save the environment. It makes her sound fierce but she's really very sweet and kind.

Gran is 70 years old. She has curly brown hair, pink cheeks and twinkly blue eyes. Her eyesight isn't very good so she has to wear glasses. She is short and a bit plump. Although she has a few wrinkles, she doesn't look very old.

Gran loves nature. She is retired, so she has lots of time to spend in her garden. She grows the most amazing vegetables! When I visit her, she lets me water them while she does other jobs around the garden.

Gran cares about the environment. She is always telling people to recycle and reuse. She also does volunteer work for Keep Australia Beautiful. She says it keeps her fit and healthy.

Another thing that Gran is good at is cooking. Her meals always taste better than Mum's, but I don't tell Mum that!

I always have a good time when I visit Gran because we do so many interesting things together. I also admire her for the great work she does for the environment. Gran is definitely one of my favourite people!

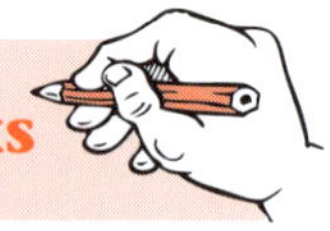

## Tasks

1. **Underline** three **adjectives** that describe Gran.
2. **Circle** the **conjunction** that links the idea of Gran's poor eyesight with her having to wear glasses.
3. **Highlight** the **adjective** that is similar in meaning to *most wonderful*.
4. **Underline** two **adjectives** that describe Gran.
5. **Circle** the **conjunction**.
6. **Highlight** Nina's **final comment** about Gran.

# Student B: Javid's draft

Javid, another student in Nina's class, is going to write a **description** of his older brother, Malik.

He starts by looking at a photo of his brother. Then he writes words and phrases to describe Malik around the photo.

straight black hair

tall and thin

wears stylish clothes

popular

has a sense of humour

studies hard

very clever

going to be a doctor

good at basketball

goes to the gym

patient

1 Javid has used lots of adjectives to describe his brother.

a List four **adjectives** that help to describe Malik's appearance.

______________________________________________

b List four **adjectives** that describe what kind of person Malik is.

______________________________________________

2 Which two things does Malik most likely do in his spare time?

______________________________________________

______________________________________________

# Writing the first draft

This is Javid's **first draft**. Read what he wrote and then answer the questions.

## My Brother, Malik

I am going to describe my brother, Malik. Malik is twenty years old. He has straight black hair. He is tall and thin. He wears stylish clothes. He goes to university. He is going to be a doctor. He is very clever. He studies hard. He is popular with his friends. He is patient. He has a sense of humour. He goes to the gym every day. He likes to play basketball.

**1** Which of these features has Javid remembered to use in his draft? Tick (✓) the correct answers.

- **a** an **introduction** to get his **reader's attention** ☐
- **b** **paragraphs** to **describe** his brother ☐
- **c** **adjectives** that **describe** his brother ☐
- **d** **present-tense verbs** ☐
- **e** **conjunctions** to **link** ideas and make his writing **flow** ☐
- **f** **sentences** that have the **correct spelling** and **punctuation** ☐
- **g** a **conclusion** that includes his **final comment** or **thought** about his brother ☐

**2** Like Nina, Javid has remembered to use present-tense verbs throughout his draft.

- **a** Which three **verbs** in the draft are formed from the base word *go*?

______________________________

- **b** Which **verb** in the draft shows that something belongs to Malik?

______________________________

**3** Which word describes someone who studies hard? Tick (✓) the correct word.

studio ☐ studious ☐ student ☐

## Step-by-step improvement plan

Javid is also going to do some practice exercises to find ways to improve his **description**. Help him complete them.

### Step 1: Start with a good introduction.

Help Javid write a good **introduction** using these words and phrases.

complain about

my friends

I'm lucky

older brothers and sisters

have a great older brother

**Hint!** First use the phrase *my friends*.

### Step 2: Link ideas with conjunctions

1. Match these **sentence** beginnings and endings. Shade the parts that belong together the same colour.

| | |
|---|---|
| **a** Malik is tall and thin and | he also works very hard. |
| **b** Malik is studying to be a doctor so | he goes to the gym every day. |
| **c** Malik is very fit because | has straight black hair. |
| **d** Malik is very clever but | he finishes university. |
| **e** Malik will stay at home with us until | he is still at university. |

2 Complete the following sentences with the correct **conjunction** from the brackets.

a (Because, Although, But) ________________ Malik has lots of work to do for university, he still has time to play basketball.

b I always go and watch (unless, when, until) ________________ Malik plays a basketball match.

c Malik goes to the gym every morning, (until, so, unless) ________________ he has other important things to do.

## Step 3: End with a good conclusion

Use these **words** and **phrases** to complete the paragraph below.

| | | |
|---|---|---|
| and | at school | hero |
| smart | kind | also |

I admire my brother because he is so ______________ and ______________. I work hard ______________________ so that one day I will ______________________ be able to go to university ____________________ become a doctor like Malik. He is my ____________________!

# Writing the final draft

Javid has started writing the **final draft** of his **description**. Complete it by filling in the missing sections, and then look in the answer section to compare what you have written with what Javid wrote.

**Hint!** Look at the practice exercises for ideas.

## My Brother

(Write the introduction.)

..........

..........

..........

..........

..........

My brother's name is Malik. (Tell how old Malik is, what he looks like and why he is fit.)

..........

..........

..........

..........

..........

Malik is studying to be a doctor, so he is still at university. He is very clever, but he also works hard. I think he will be a very good doctor because he is so kind and patient.

Although Malik has lots of university work to do, he still has time to play basketball. He is very good at it. He is also very popular and has lots of friends.

(Write the conclusion)

..........

..........

..........

..........

..........

..........

# Your turn

Write a **description** of about one page on one of the following. Use your own paper for this activity.

**Writing Checklist** Make sure you: ✓

- start with an interesting **introduction**. ☐
- use **paragraphs** to describe the person you are writing about. ☐
- use interesting **adjectives** to describe the person. ☐
- use **conjunctions** to link ideas. ☐
- write in the **present tense**. ☐
- end with a **conclusion** that contains a **final comment** about the person you are describing. ☐

**Tip** Use **Nina's final draft** on page 30 and **Javid's final draft** on page 35 to help you write your description.

Go to WORD BANK page 105 for useful vocabulary

1. Write a description of someone you know well.

   Use Nina and Javid's descriptions as models.

2. Imagine you know one of the people pictured below. Write a description of him or her.

3. Write a description of someone you would like to have as a friend. The person can be real or imaginary.

# Unit 4 Writing to persuade—expositions

## Looking at expositions

An **exposition** aims to **persuade** people to agree with an **opinion** or **belief**.

Most of us have tried to persuade people to do things or agree with us in our everyday conversations. Sometimes we might want to give a speech or write a letter, article or blog to try to persuade others.

An **exposition** should have:

- an **opening paragraph** that states your main **opinion**.
  For example: *I think that cats make better pets than dogs.*
- **arguments** or reasons for your opinion.
  For example: *Firstly, cats are not as noisy as dogs.*
- a **conclusion** that **repeats** your opinion and **refers back** briefly to your arguments.
  For example: *As you can see from the reasons I've given, cats definitely make better pets than dogs.*

1 Which of the following two sentences expresses an **opinion**?

**a** Lots of students bring their mobile phones to school. ☐

**b** I don't think students should bring their mobile phones to school. ☐

2 Which child is trying to persuade his or her mother to buy him or her a computer game?

**a** I wonder if this store has the new computer game. I'll go and have a look. ☐

**b** Just think, Mum, you won't hear or see me for hours if you buy me this computer game. ☐

# Student A: Gabriel's draft

The students in Gabriel's Year 3 class at North Park Public School each have to write a **letter** to a group of people to persuade them to do something.

Gabriel decides to write to the Year 2s at North Park Infants' School to persuade them to come to North Park Public School in Year 3.

He starts by jotting down some ideas.

**Arguments**:

1 excellent teachers

2 cool playground

3 great library

**Details to add to arguments**:

amazing playground equipment

interesting lessons

teachers kind and helpful

magazines and newspapers

kind and caring principal

lots of books

shady trees

teachers take us on excursions

basketball court

library the heart of the school

Complete the table below with the correct details from Gabriel's notes.

| Argument | Details to add to arguments |
|---|---|
| 1 excellent teachers | |
| 2 cool playground | |
| 3 great library | |

# Writing the first draft

This is Gabriel's **first draft**. Read what he wrote and then answer the questions.

Dear Year 2s

Next year you will have to go to another school. You should come to North Park Public School, for the following reasons.

We have very good teachers. They are caring and helpful. They take us on excursions. They make our lessons interesting.

Our school has big grounds. There are lots of shady trees. The playground equipment is amazing. We have a basketball court. We have a vegetable garden.

We have a great library. It has lots of books. There are newspapers and magazines in the library.

That's why you should come to North Park Public School.

From Gabriel (a Year 3 student at North Park Public School)

1. A good **exposition** should contain the following features. Tick (✓) the ones that Gabriel has used.

   - **a** an **introduction** that states the main **opinion** ☐
   - **b** **arguments** or **reasons** for the opinion ☐
   - **c** **thinking** and **feeling verbs** (e.g. *believe* or *know*) ☐
   - **d** **present-tense verbs** (e.g. *is* or *have*) ☐
   - **e** **connectives** to link **arguments** (e.g. *Firstly* or *In addition*) ☐
   - **f** a separate **paragraph** for each argument ☐
   - **g** **correct spelling** and **punctuation** ☐
   - **h** a **conclusion** that **repeats** the opinion and **refers back** briefly to the arguments ☐

2. Which **adjective** has Gabriel used to describe:

   - **a** the teachers' lessons? ______________________
   - **b** the trees in the playground? ______________________
   - **c** the playground equipment? ______________________

3. What is the **contraction** *That's* short for in Gabriel's draft? Tick (✓) the correct words.

   That was ☐ | That is ☐ | That as ☐

# Step-by-step improvement plan

Help Gabriel complete these practice exercises to find ways to improve his **letter**.

## Step 1: Use thinking and feeling verbs

**Thinking** and **feeling verbs** are verbs that tell what's going on in your head. For example: *I* **know**, *I* **believe**.

In a persuasive text, they help you to **express opinions** and **emotions**.

Complete the sentences below with a thinking or feeling **verb** from the box. Use each verb once.

| | | | | | |
|---|---|---|---|---|---|
| thinks | decided | know | love | hope | like |

1. I ____________ all of the teachers at North Park Public School and I ____________ you will too.
2. I ____________ to see you all at North Park Public School next year.
3. Everyone at North Park Public School ____________ that it is a great school.
4. Have you ____________ which school to go to next year?
5. I really ____________ my school!

## Step 2: Link ideas with connectives

**Connectives** are words and phrases that **link** ideas in a text (e.g. *Firstly* or *Then*). They help make our writing flow.

Use the **connectives** from the box to complete this passage. Use each connective once.

| | | | | | |
|---|---|---|---|---|---|
| Firstly | Secondly | Finally | so | also | In addition |

I think that North Park Public School is an excellent school for the following reasons.

____________________, we have amazing teachers who are always ready to help us. We ____________________ have a kind and caring principal. ____________________, we have big grounds to play in. ____________________, we have a basketball court that we're allowed to use during the lunch break.

______________________________, we have a great library that is packed with books. Everyone at the school is very friendly, ______________________________ the students are all happy.

## Step 3: Ending with a strong conclusion

The **conclusion** is the final paragraph. It should **repeat** your opinion and **refer back briefly** to your arguments.

Gabriel is not completely happy with his conclusion, so he has written two different endings.

1. Which **ending** repeats his main opinion and refers back briefly to his arguments?

**A** North Park is definitely an excellent school. I know you will like it here. You should come here in Year 3. ☐

**B** I have given you many reasons why you should come to North Park Public School next year. I am sure you will agree that it's a great school! ☐

2. Choose the best **ending** to complete the following sentence.

   Now that you know how great North Park Public School is,

   **a** maybe you will tell all your friends about it. ☐

   **b** I am sure you will all decide to come here next year. ☐

   **c** perhaps you will want to go to another school. ☐

3. Now use the ideas in numbers 1 and 2 to write a strong **conclusion** for Gabriel's letter.

______________________________

______________________________

______________________________

______________________________

______________________________

______________________________

# Writing the final draft

This is Gabriel's **final draft**. Read the comments about her **letter** on the left, and do the tasks on the right.

## Comments

*The* **introduction** *should contain your main argument.*

*Giving reasons for your* **arguments** *helps to persuade your reader.*

*Using* **connectives** *to link your arguments makes your writing flow.*

*Using a separate* **paragraph** *for each argument makes your text easier to understand.*

*A good* **conclusion** *wraps up your arguments.*

---

Dear Year 2s

Next year you will have to go to another school. I think you should come to North Park Public School, for the following reasons.

Firstly, we have amazing teachers who are always ready to help us. Their lessons are interesting and they take us on excursions to help us understand the things we are learning about. For example, we visited the zoo to learn how we can help save endangered animals.

Secondly, we have a kind and caring principal and friendly students, so everyone at our school is very happy.

In addition, we have big grounds to play in. We have great playground equipment and a canteen where we can buy healthy, delicious food and drinks. We also have a basketball court that we're allowed to use at lunchtime.

Another interesting part of our playground is the vegetable garden. It helps us learn how to grow our own food.

Finally, we have a brilliant library. It is packed with books, magazines and newspapers. Our librarian says it's the heart of the school.

Now that you know how great North Park Public School is, I am sure that you will all decide to come here next year.

From Gabriel (a Year 3 student at NPPS)

---

## Tasks

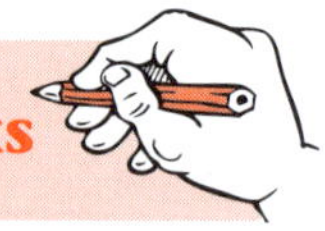

1. **Underline** the **opinion**.
2. **Highlight** one **reason** why the teachers are amazing.
3. **Circle** one **connective**.
4. **Underline** two **connectives**.
5. **Highlight** the **reason** that the library is brilliant.
6. **Underline** the **word** that shows that Gabriel is certain about something.

# Student B: Sienna's draft

Sienna, another Year 3 student, is going to write to some imaginary cousins who will soon be moving to her city. She is going to persuade them to find a house in Eastlands, the suburb she lives in.

She also starts by writing down her ideas.

**Arguments**:

1 lots of places to have fun and relax

2 lots of shops

3 good public transport system

**Details to add to arguments**:

regular bus service

big supermarket

lots of restaurants and cafes

two big parks

train station

big hardware store

Help Sienna organise her ideas by filling in the argument that goes with the supporting details.

| Argument | Supporting details |
| --- | --- |
| 1 | big supermarket<br>big hardware store |
| 2 | train station<br>regular bus service |
| 3 | two big parks<br>lots of restaurants and cafes |

# Writing the first draft

This is Sienna's **first draft**. Read what she wrote and then answer the questions.

> Dear Paula and Tessa
>
> I am so excited that you're moving to Melbourne. You must come and live in Eastlands when you get here. It's a great place to live, for many reasons.
>
> Eastlands has lots of shops. It has a big supermarket and a big hardware store. It has lots of other little shops.
>
> Eastlands has a good public transport system. There is a regular bus service into the city. The train station is in the middle of the suburb.
>
> There are lots of places to relax and have fun in Eastlands. It has two big parks. It has lots of cafes and restaurants.
>
> You will like living in Eastlands.
>
> Love, Sienna

1 Which of these features has Sienna remembered to use in her draft? Tick (✓) the correct answers.

- a an **introduction** that states the main opinion ☐
- b **arguments** or **reasons** for the opinion ☐
- c **thinking** and **feeling verbs** ☐
- d **present-tense verbs** ☐
- e **connectives** to link **arguments** ☐
- f a separate **paragraph** for each argument ☐
- g **correct spelling** and **punctuation** ☐
- h a **conclusion** that **repeats** the opinion and **refers back** briefly to the arguments ☐

2 Which **adjective** has Sienna used to describe:

a her feelings at the thought of her cousins moving to Melbourne?

______________________________

b Eastlands' public transport system? ____________________

c the bus service into the city? ____________________

3 List two **contractions** (shortened forms of words) that Sienna has used in her draft.

______________ ______________

4 Write the **contractions** for:

a There is ________________

b You will ________________

## Step-by-step improvement plan

Sienna also needs to work on her **letter** to make it more interesting. Help her complete these exercises.

### Step 1: Use thinking and feeling verbs

Sienna has written these sentences. Use a thinking or feeling **verb** from the box to fill in each sentence. Use each word once.

**Hint!** Read through all the sentences before making your choice.

| | | | |
|---|---|---|---|
| imagine | think | enjoy | believe |
| wonder | suppose | know | |

1 I ________________ that you should live in Eastlands.

2 I ________________ you could live anywhere in Melbourne, but I ________________ you should live near us.

3 I ________________ if you ________________ what a great place Eastlands is.

4 I can't ________________ living anywhere else!

5 I really ________________ living in Eastlands.

### Step 2: Linking ideas with connectives

1 Underline the **connective** in brackets that correctly completes each sentence.

a Eastlands has a large supermarket and hardware store, (as well as/in addition) lots of other interesting shops.

b There is a regular bus service into the city and there is (therefore/also) a train station in the middle of the suburb.

c Eastlands has lots of places where you can relax and have fun, (such as/however) parks, cafes and restaurants.

d There are lots of things for children to do in Eastlands; (nevertheless/for example), it has a great skateboard park and a large public swimming pool.

e (As a result, In addition), Eastlands is close to the beach.

2 Use information from Sienna's notes and draft to help you complete the following sentences.

a There are lots of things for children to do in Eastlands, therefore

______________________________

b Eastlands is close to the city; however, ______________________________

______________________________

## Step 3: Ending with a good conclusion

Sienna has written two **conclusions** that she could use to wrap up her exposition. Which one repeats her main opinion and refers back to her arguments?

1 a

I really think you should come and live in Eastlands. We've lived here for a long time. I really like living here, and so will you. ☐

b

I am sure my arguments have persuaded you that Eastlands is a great suburb to live in. Just think of the fun we'll have if you live close by! ☐

2 Complete these sentences to give Sienna's exposition a different **conclusion**.

Now that you know what a great place ______________________________

______________________________,

I am sure you will ______________________________

______________________________.

I can't wait ______________________________

______________________________.

# Writing the final draft

Sienna has started writing the **final draft** of her **letter**. Help her complete it by filling in the missing sections, and then look in the answers section to compare what you have written with what she wrote.

**Hint!** Look at the practice exercises for ideas.

Dear Paula and Tessa

I am so excited you are moving to Melbourne! When you get here, I believe you should live in Eastlands. I am sure you will want to when I tell you what a great place it is.

Firstly, you can buy anything you need in Eastlands, from food to furniture. There is a large supermarket and hardware store, as well as many other interesting shops. But that's just one of the reasons I like living here.

Secondly, Eastlands has an excellent public transport system, so it is easy to get to and from the city. We have a regular bus service and there is a train station in the middle of the suburb. Also, the trains and buses are always on time!

Finally, **(Write about the places where they can relax and have fun in Eastlands.)**

**(Write the conclusion.)**

Love, Sienna

## Your turn

Write an **exposition** of about a page on one of the following. Use your own paper for this activity.

**Writing Checklist** Make sure your exposition includes: ✓

- an **introduction** that states the writer's main **opinion** in an interesting way. ☐
- **arguments** or **reasons** for the opinion. ☐
- **thinking** and **feeling verbs**. ☐
- **present-tense verbs**. ☐
- **connectives** to link **arguments** and ideas. ☐
- **paragraphs** to organise your writing. ☐
- a **conclusion** that **repeats** the opinion and **refers back** briefly to the arguments. ☐

**Tip** Use **Gabriel's final draft** on page 42 and **Sienna's final draft** on page 47 to help you write your persuasive text.

Go to WORD BANK page 105 for useful vocabulary

1. Write a letter to a group of students who are undecided about which school to attend in Year 3. Persuade them that they should come to your school.

**Tip** Look back at how Gabriel wrote his letter.

2. Write a letter to imaginary friends or relatives who will soon be moving to your town or city. Persuade them to come and live in your suburb.

**Tip** Look back at how Sienna wrote her letter.

3. Write an exposition entitled *Why every child needs a pet.*

   Some key words you could use are *love, companion* and *responsibility.*

4. Write an exposition entitled *Why every child should learn to ride a bicycle.*

   Key words you could use are *fun, exercise* and *confidence.*

# Unit 5 Writing a narrative

## Looking at narratives

A **narrative** tells a story about a real or imaginary event in an **entertaining** and interesting way. There are many different kinds of narratives, like fairy tales, mysteries and fantasy stories.

A **narrative** should have:

- an **orientation**, or **beginning**, that tells your reader **who**, **where**, **when** and **what**.
- a build-up to a **complication** or **problem** that has to be **resolved**.
- a **series of events** that result from the **complication**.
- an **ending** or **resolution**, in which the problem is **solved**.

Read the following short **narrative** and then answer the questions.

There were once two naughty little polar bears who were always leaving their mother. One day they decided to explore an iceberg. It was close to shore, so they could easily reach it.

The little bears were having a great time frolicking about on the ice. But suddenly it started to move.

The furry little creatures were terrified! They screamed at the top of their squeaky little voices.

Luckily their mother heard them. She dived into the water and swam out to get them. In no time at all, she had her inquisitive little cubs safely back on shore. They promised never to leave her side again!

1. Look at the **orientation**.
   - a Who is the story about? ______
   - b Where does the story take place? ______
   - c What were the polar bears going to do? ______
2. What was the **complication**, or problem, that had to be solved?
   ______
   ______
3. What did the polar bears do when they saw they were in trouble?
   ______
4. How was the **problem** solved? ______
   ______
   ______

# Student A: Samara's draft

Students in Samara's Year 3 class each have to choose a rhyme and turn it into a **narrative**. Samara is going to base her narrative on this funny version of *Row, row, row your boat.*

Row, row, row your boat,

Gently down the stream.

If you see a crocodile,

Don't forget to scream

The first thing Samara does is plan her narrative.

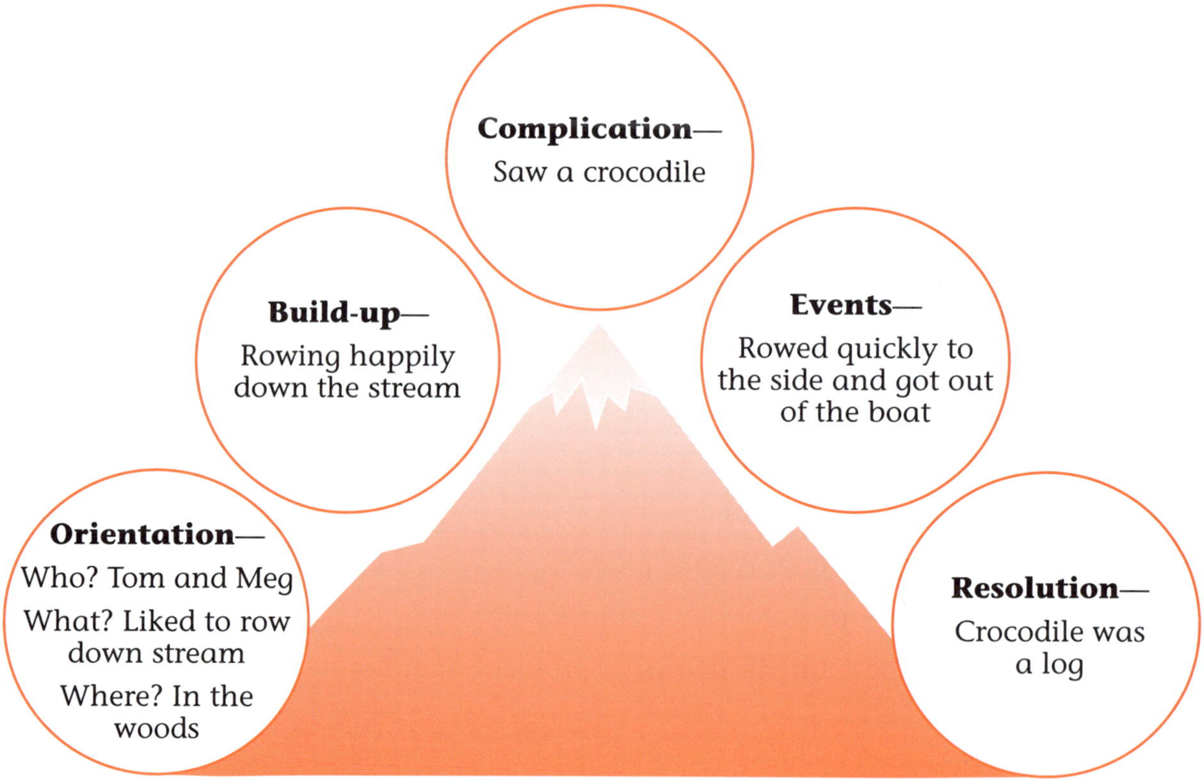


**1** Which **sentence** might Samara use to show what Tom and Meg felt when they saw the crocodile?

They felt sad. ☐ They felt silly. ☐ They were terrified. ☐

**2** Which **sentence** might she use to show what the children felt when they saw that the crocodile was a log?

They felt sad. ☐ They felt silly. ☐ They were scared. ☐

## Writing the first draft

This is Samara's **first draft**. Read what she wrote and then answer the questions.

### The Crocodile

Two children named Meg and Tom lived in the woods. They lived near a stream. They liked to row their boat down the stream.

One day they were rowing down the stream. Tom was rowing and Meg had her hand in the water.

Suddenly Tom saw a crocodile in the water. He told Meg to take her hand out of the water. Meg was scared but Tom said not to worry.

He rowed the boat to the side and they got out. They watched the crocodile swim past. Imagine how silly they felt when they saw it was just a log!

1. A good **narrative** should contain the following features. Tick (✓) the ones that Samara has used.

   a. a clear **orientation** that tells **who**, **what**, **when** and **where** ☐
   b. an interesting **complication** ☐
   c. a **series of events** divided into paragraphs ☐
   d. **descriptive verbs** (e.g. using words like *spy, spot* or *notice* instead of *see*) ☐
   e. **past-tense verbs** (e.g. *lived* or *watched*) ☐
   f. interesting **information** and **detail** about the events ☐
   g. **correct spelling** and **punctuation** ☐
   h. an interesting **resolution** that shows how the problem is solved ☐

2. Find the **past tense** of these verbs in Samara's narrative and write them in the spaces.

   a. has ______________ b. see ______________ c. tell ______________
   d. say ______________ e. feel ______________

3. Which is the best **description** of a crocodile? Tick (✓) the correct sentence.

   It's an animal that lives in the water and lays eggs. ☐
   It's an animal that lives mainly in the water and looks like an alligator. ☐
   It's an animal that can live on the land or in the water. ☐

# Step-by-step improvement plan

Help Samara complete these practice exercises to find ways to make her **narrative** more interesting.

## Step 1: Add interest with descriptive verbs

**Verbs** can tell us **what** people and things are **doing**.
For example: *The children* ***were rowing*** *down the stream.*

Some verbs are more descriptive than others.
For example, *stare* is more descriptive than *look* because it tells us *how* a person looks at something.

Using **descriptive verbs** in a narrative makes your story more **interesting** to read.

Use a **descriptive verb** from the box to replace the underlined words in these sentences.

| trailing | twittering | swishing | peeping |
|---|---|---|---|

1. The birds were making a noise in the trees. ______________________
2. The water was flowing around them. ______________________
3. Meg was holding her hand in the water. ______________________
4. Two eyes and a snout were looking out of the water ______________________

## Step 2: Add colour and interest with similes

**Similes** compare one thing to something else using the words ***like*** or ***as***.
For example: *The water was* ***as*** *cold* ***as*** *ice.*
*The water felt* ***like*** *ice.*

Using **similes** helps the reader create mind pictures of the people, places and events you are writing about. Like descriptive verbs, they add interest to your text.

Complete these **similes** that can show how frightened someone is. Think about what makes the most sense and creates the best picture. Put a circle around the correct word.

1. Her eyes were as big as (pearls, saucers, ants).
2. She was shaking like a (leaf, monkey, vegetable).
3. Her legs felt like (gold, chairs, jelly).
4. She went as white as a (blanket, crow, sheet).
5. Her heart was fluttering like a (butterfly, spider, kitten).

## Step 3: Bring the characters to life with dialogue

**Dialogue** is the actual words characters use in a text. It can help to bring your characters to life.

**Hint!** Be careful! Using too much dialogue can spoil your narrative.

**Reminder!** It is important that you punctuate dialogue correctly.

- Use **speech marks** (“”) around the actual words that a character says, **including** any punctuation.
- Use a **capital letter** when someone speaks for the first time, even if the first spoken word comes after a comma.
- Start a **new paragraph** when a new character starts speaking.

For example: “We have to get to the side as quickly as possible,” said Tom.
Meg asked, “Why? What’s wrong?”

1. Which sentence below shows better that Tom is worried?
   - **a** “You’d better get your hand out of the water, Meg.” ☐
   - **b** “Meg! Get your hand out of the water!” ☐
2. Which sentence shows that Tom is calm?
   - **a** “Don’t worry, Meg, I won’t let it get us.” ☐
   - **b** “What are we going to do, Meg?” ☐
3. Underline the exact words Tom and Meg say.
   - **a** Tom shouted, “Meg! Get your hand out of the water!”
   - **b** “Why?” she asked.
   - **c** “A c-c-crocodile,” stuttered Tom. “Over there!”
   - **d** “Don’t worry, Meg,” said Tom, “I won’t let it get us.”
4. Fill in the missing **speech marks** in the following sentences.
   - **a** Tom said, I really thought that was a crocodile.
   - **b** Oh, Tom, said Meg, you gave me such a fright.
   - **c** Let’s not tell anyone how silly we were, said Tom.

# Writing the final draft

This is Samara's **final draft**. Read the comments about her **narrative** on the left, and do the tasks on the right.

**Comments**

*A clear* ***orientation*** *tells the reader who, what, when and where.*

*Using* ***descriptive verbs*** *makes the story more interesting to read.*

*An interesting* ***complication*** *draws the reader in.*

*Using* ***dialogue*** *brings the characters to life.*

*The* ***resolution*** *solves the problem and wraps up the story.*

## The Crocodile

Two children named Tom and Meg lived in the woods. Nearby was a peaceful stream. The children liked to row gently down the stream in their little boat.

One sunny morning they were out in their boat. Tom was rowing and Meg was trailing her hand in the water. They were so happy. They could hear the birds twittering in the trees and the water swishing around them.

Suddenly Tom shouted, "Meg! Get your hand out of the water!"

Meg looked at him in surprise. "Why?" she asked.

"A c-c-crocodile," stuttered Tom. "Over there!"

Meg looked to where Tom was pointing. She could just make out two beady eyes and a long snout peeping out of the water. She looked at Tom. Her eyes were as big as saucers.

"Don't worry, Meg," said Tom, "I won't let it get us."

Tom steered the boat towards the bank. Quickly, the children jumped out and pulled the boat away from the edge. They watched from a safe distance as the crocodile swam past. Imagine how silly they felt when they saw it was just a log!

**Tasks**

1. **Highlight** the **words** that tell us where the story happened.
2. **Circle** three **descriptive verbs**.
3. **Underline** the exact **words** Tom says.
4. **Highlight** the **simile**.
5. **Highlight** the **word** that tells how the children jumped out of the boat.

# Student B: Aiden's draft

Aiden, another Year 3 student, is going to base his **narrative** on the rhyme about Humpty Dumpty.

Humpty Dumpty sat
on a wall,
Humpty Dumpty had
a great fall.
All the king's horses
and all the king's men
Couldn't put Humpty
together again.

Aiden also starts by planning his narrative.

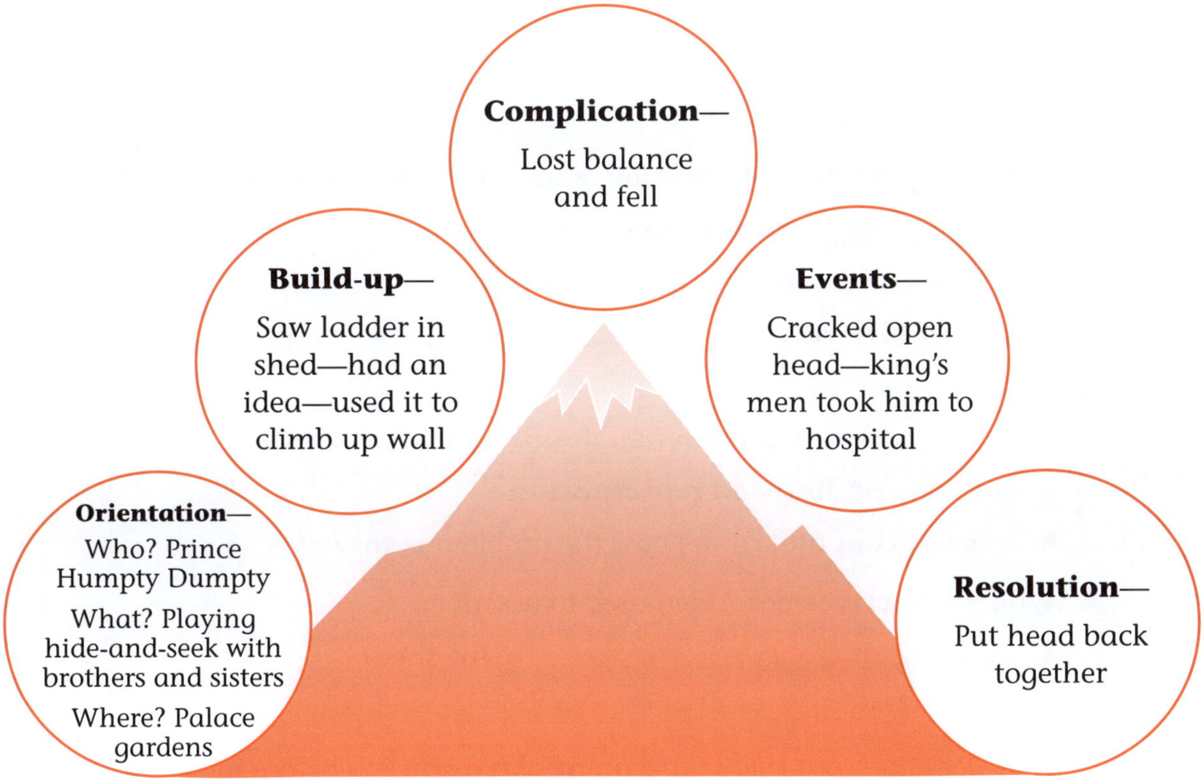


Use **words** and **phrases** from Aiden's plan to complete the following sentences.

1. Humpty got the idea to climb up the wall when ______________________________

   ______________________________

2. Luckily, the doctor was able ______________________________

   ______________________________

# Writing the first draft

This is Aiden's **first draft**. Read what he wrote and then answer the questions.

## Humpty's Great Fall

One morning Humpty was playing hide-and-seek with his brothers and sisters in the palace gardens.

Humpty was hiding in the dusty shed. He saw a ladder. He was a curious boy. He had an idea.

He asked his brothers, Gumpty and Lumpty, to help him carry the ladder to the great stone wall. He said he was going to climb to the top.

Gumpty and Lumpty held the ladder. Humpty climbed to the top. The ladder started to shake. Humpty lost his balance. He fell.

Gumpty and Lumpty called for help. The king's men came quickly. Humpty's head was cracked open!

1 Which of these features has Aiden remembered to include in his draft? Tick (✓) the correct answers.

- a a clear **orientation** that tells **who**, **what**, **when** and **where** ☐
- b an interesting **complication** ☐
- c a **series of events** divided into **paragraphs** ☐
- d **descriptive verbs** ☐
- e **past-tense verbs** ☐
- f interesting **information** and **detail** about the events ☐
- g **correct spelling** and **punctuation** ☐
- h a **resolution** that shows how the problem is **solved** ☐

2 Which **adjectives** has Aiden used to describe:

a Humpty? ____________ b the shed? ____________

c the wall? ____________

3 Why does the word *king's* have an **apostrophe** ( ' ) before the ***s***? Tick (✓) the correct answer.

to show that there was more than one king ☐

to show that the men belonged to the king ☐

# Step-by-step improvement plan

Aiden is also going to do some practice exercises to find ways to improve his **narrative**. Help him complete them.

## Step 1: Add interest with descriptive verbs

Replace each of the underlined **verbs** below with a more descriptive one from the list.

- raced
- noticed
- tumbling
- clambered
- dragged
- wobble
- peer

1. Humpty saw ______________ a ladder in the corner.
2. The little princes carried ______________ the ladder to the wall.
3. Quickly Humpty climbed ______________ up the ladder.
4. Humpty was just about to look ______________ over the wall.
5. The ladder started to shake ______________.
6. Humpty lost his balance and came falling ______________ down.
7. The king's men ran ______________ to help the little prince.

## Step 2: Bring the characters to life with dialogue

1. In which sentence is the speaker asking a **question**?

a. Gumpty asked, "What are you going to do with this ladder?" ☐

b. Humpty replied, "I'm going to climb to the top of the wall to see what's on the other side." ☐

c. "Wow!" said Gumpty and Lumpty. ☐

2. Which example of **dialogue** shows that Gumpty and Lumpty were worried about Humpty?

a. "Poor Humpty has had a great fall." ☐

b. "Help! Help! Humpty's had a terrible accident!" ☐

3 Fill in the **speech marks** in the following sentences.

a Will he be all right? asked Gumpty and Lumpty.

b The doctor replied, He's going to be just fine!

## Step 3: End with an interesting resolution

The **resolution** is the final paragraph or two of the narrative. It should show **how the problem is solved**. It should also wrap your story up in an interesting way.

Use the **words** and **phrases** on the notes to help you write a more interesting ending for Aiden's narrative.

- rushed him to hospital
- stitch Humpty's head back together
- as good as new
- lifted him onto a horse
- Carefully

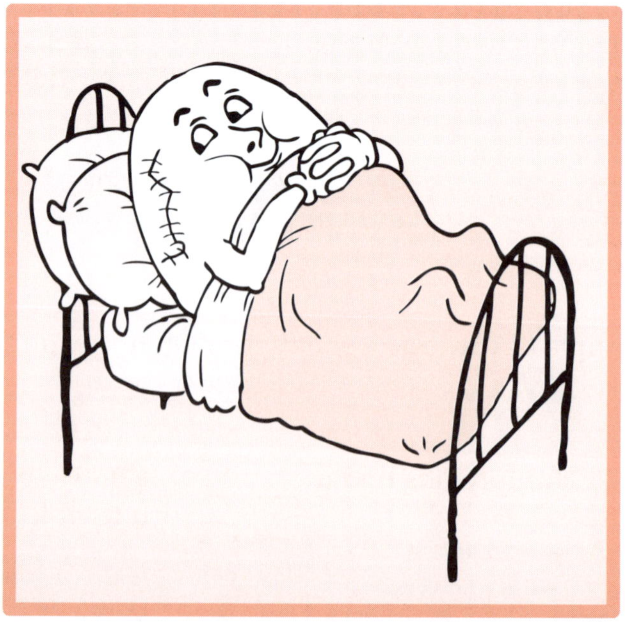

# Writing the final draft

Aiden has started writing the **final draft** of his **narrative**. Help him complete it by filling in the missing sections, and then look in the answers section to compare what you have written with what Aiden wrote.

**Hint!** Look at Aiden's first draft and practice exercises for ideas.

## Humpty's Great Fall!

One morning Humpty was playing hide-and-seek with his brothers and sisters in the palace gardens. Of all the king's children, Humpty was the most curious.

While he was hiding inside a dusty shed, he noticed a ladder in the corner. It gave him an idea.

Later that morning, Humpty asked his brothers, Gumpty and Lumpty, to help him carry the ladder to the great stone wall.

**(Write the dialogue that tells what Gumpty and Lumpty asked Humpty about the ladder and Humpty's reply.)**

..............................................................................................................................

..............................................................................................................................

..............................................................................................................................

..............................................................................................................................

..............................................................................................................................

..............................................................................................................................

The three little princes dragged the ladder to the wall. Gumpty and Lumpty held it steady while Humpty clambered to the top. He was just about to peer over the wall when the ladder started to wobble. Humpty lost his balance and came tumbling down. He hit the ground with a loud thud.

"Help! Help!" cried Gumpty and Lumpty. "Humpty's had a terrible accident!"

The king's men raced to help the little prince. They found him with his head cracked open!

**(Write the final paragraph in which the problem is solved.)**

..............................................................................................................................

..............................................................................................................................

..............................................................................................................................

..............................................................................................................................

## Your turn

Write a **narrative** of about a page on one of the following. Use your own paper for this activity.

**Writing Checklist** Make sure your narrative contains: ✓

- a **title**. ☐
- an **orientation** that captures the reader's attention and sets the scene by telling **who**, **what**, **where** and **when**. ☐
- an interesting **complication** or problem. ☐
- a **series of events** divided into paragraphs. ☐
- **interesting adjectives** and **descriptive verbs**. ☐
- interesting **information** and **detail** about the events. ☐
- a **resolution** in which the problem is solved. ☐

**Tip** Use **Samara's final draft** on page 54 and **Aiden's final draft** on page 59 to help you write your narrative.

Go to WORD BANK pages 105–106 for useful vocabulary

1. Write a narrative that starts like this:

   *Miss Muffet's favourite thing to do on a sunny afternoon was to sit on her little stool in the garden. Once she was comfortable, her mother would bring her a bowl of cottage cheese to eat.*

   Continue the narrative, describing how a spider came and sat beside Miss Muffet and frightened her away.

2. Turn the following nursery rhyme into a narrative.

   *Jack and Jill*
   *Went up the hill*
   *To fetch a pail of water,*
   *Jack fell down*
   *And broke his crown*
   *And Jill came tumbling after.*

   *Up Jack got*
   *And home did trot*
   *As fast as he could caper,*
   *Went to bed*
   *To mend his head*
   *With vinegar and brown paper.*

# Unit 6 Writing an information report

## Looking at information reports

An **information report** gives facts and information about a subject.

You will often have to write reports for your different school subjects. For example, you might have to write about:

- plants and animals (e.g. eucalyptus trees and wombats).
- technology (e.g. computers and motor cars).
- people, countries and cultures (e.g. the Ancient Egyptians and China).

An **information report** should have:

- an **introduction** that includes a **short definition** or **description** of your subject.
- **paragraphs** that give **factual information** about your subject. These paragraphs may be organised under subheadings.
- a **conclusion** that rounds off your report.

**Hint!** We often use **diagrams** or **charts** in information reports.

Read the short information report below and then answer the questions.

Kookaburras are native Australian birds. They are part of the kingfisher family.

Kookaburras have short, thick bodies and long, sharp bills. They have brown, black and white feathers. There are blue patches on some of the feathers.

Kookaburras are carnivorous (meat-eating) birds. They feed on small animals such as insects, lizards and worms.

Kookaburras make a laughing call. They can be heard mainly in the early morning or around sunset.

According to an Aboriginal legend, the kookaburra's call lets the great sky spirits know when to light the great fire, or sun, in the morning and when to put it out in the evening.

1 What does the **introduction** tell us about kookaburras? Tick (✓) the correct answers.

a where kookaburras are found ☐ b the sound kookaburras make ☐

c what kookaburras look like ☐

d which group of birds kookaburras belong to ☐

2 What information about kookaburras is in the three middle **paragraphs**? Tick (✓) the correct answers.

a how long they live ☐ b what they look like ☐ c where they live ☐

d what they eat ☐ e what they sound like ☐ f when they breed ☐

# Student A: Rashid's draft

Each student in Rashid's Year 3 class has to write an **information report** about his or her favourite fruit. Rashid is going to write about the apple.

First, he collected photographs of apples and apple trees. Then he jotted down facts about the appearance and different types of apples, how and where they are grown and why they are good for us.

Nutritional value—Healthy—contain important vitamins and minerals

Varieties (types)—Granny Smith, Red Delicious, Pink Lady, Fuji, Gala, Golden Delicious

People have been eating apples for thousands of years

Colours—Green, yellow, pink, orange-red, dark red

Shape and size—Round, no bigger than a tennis ball

Flowers appear in spring—pollinated by insects—apples grow from the flowers—ripen in the autumn

Member of the rose family

Granny Smith comes from Australia—named after Maria Ann Smith who grew the first one in Sydney in 1868

More than 7000 varieties in the world

Grown in all Australian states but mainly in New South Wales, Victoria and Tasmania

Help Rashid answer these questions. Use full sentences.

1. Why are apples good for us? ______________________

______________________

______________________

2. Where in Australia are apples grown? ______________________

______________________

______________________

# Writing the first draft

This is Rashid's **first draft**. Read what he wrote and then answer the questions.

> ## Apples
>
> **Introduction**
>
> Apples are my favourite fruit.
>
> **Appearance**
>
> Most apples are round. They are about the size of a tennis ball. They are lots of different colours, like green and red.
>
> **Where apples are grown**
>
> Apples grow all around the world.
>
> **Nutritional value**
>
> Apples are good for us. They keep us healthy. I think everyone should eat more apples.
>
> **Interesting facts**
>
> Australia was the first country to grow Granny Smith apples. There are more than 7000 kinds of apples.

**1** A good **information report** should contain the following features. Tick (✓) the ones that Rashid has used.

- **a** an **introduction** that includes a short **definition** or **description** of the subject ☐
- **b** **paragraphs** that give **detailed information** about the subject ☐
- **c** **subheadings** to organise the **paragraphs** ☐
- **d** only **facts**, not opinions ☐
- **e** **technical** or special **language** that refers specifically to the subject (e.g. *Granny Smith* or *pollinate)* ☐
- **f** **present-tense verbs** (e.g. *are* or *grow*) ☐
- **g** **correct spelling** and **punctuation** ☐
- **h** a **conclusion** that **rounds off** the report ☐

**2** Which **adjectives** has Rashid used to describe:

- **a** the shape of an apple? ______________________________
- **b** the colours of an apple? ______________________________

# Step-by-step improvement plan

Rashid is going to do these practice exercises to find ways to improve his **information report**. Help him complete them.

## Step 1: Start with a good introduction

The **introduction** is the first paragraph. It should include a **short definition** or **description** of the subject.

Use the following words and phrases to help Rashid write a better **introduction** for his report.

an edible fruit

means we can eat it

part of rose family

______________________________

______________________________

______________________________

______________________________

## Step 2: Add detail to paragraphs

A **paragraph** is a **group of sentences** about one thing. Some very short paragraphs may contain only one or two sentences.

To keep your reader's attention, your paragraphs should contain interesting **detail**.

Look at Rashid's notes again and then complete the following **sentences**. Remember to add as much detail as possible.

1. Apples come in lots of different colours. They can be ______________________________

______________________________

2. There are many different types of apple. Some of the most common varieties are

______________________________

______________________________

3. Apples are grown throughout Australia, but especially in ______________________________

______________________________

4. Granny Smith apples were first grown in Australia, but today ______________________________

______________________________

## Step 3: State facts, not opinions

A **fact** is something that can be **proved to be true**.
For example: *An apple is a fruit.*

An **opinion** is a **personal view** that may or may not be true.
For example: *I think apples are more delicious than bananas.*

An information report should contain only facts, not opinions.

1. Which sentences are **opinions**? Tick (✓) the correct answers.
   - a Apples contain vitamins and minerals. ☐
   - b Everybody loves apples. ☐
   - c Roses are the most beautiful of all the flowers. ☐
   - d An apple is part of the rose family. ☐
   - e Most apples have a round shape. ☐
   - f I think red apples are nicer than green apples. ☐
2. Rashid has expressed two **opinions** in his draft. Find them and underline them.
3. Now write a simple fact about a fruit you enjoy eating.

   For example: *An orange is a citrus fruit.*

   ______________________________________________

   ______________________________________________

4. The sentences below are about the picture. Three of them are **facts** and one is an **opinion**. Tick (✓) the **facts**.

   a Apples can be pressed to make juice. ☐

   b Apples have thin skins. ☐

   c Apples are the healthiest of all snacks. ☐

   d Apples have pips (seeds) inside them. ☐

# Writing the final draft

This is Rashid's **final draft**. Read the comments about his **report** on the left, and do the tasks on the right.

## Comments

*A good* ***introduction*** *gives a brief description of the subject.*

*Using* ***subheadings*** *tells your reader what the paragraph is about.*

*Stating* ***facts****, not opinions, gives your reader reliable information.*

*The* ***conclusion*** *rounds off the report with some interesting information about your subject.*

## Apples

### Introduction

An apple is an edible fruit. That means we can eat it. Apples are part of the rose family.

### Appearance

Apples come in different shapes, sizes and colours. They mostly have a round shape, but their skins can be green, yellow, pink, orange-red or dark red. They are usually no bigger than a tennis ball.

### Varieties

There are over 7000 different kinds of apple throughout the world. The most popular varieties in Australia are the Granny Smith, the Red Delicious, the Pink Lady, the Golden Delicious, the Gala and the Fuji.

### How apples grow

Apples grow on trees. Small white flowers appear on the trees in the spring. Insects pollinate the flowers and the apples grow from the flowers. The apples are picked in the autumn.

### Where apples are grown in Australia

Apples are grown in all of the states, but mainly in New South Wales, Victoria and Tasmania.

### Nutritional value

Apples are a healthy snack. They contain vitamins and minerals that are good for us.

### Interesting facts about apples

The Granny Smith apple was named after Maria Ann Smith, who lived in Sydney, Australia, in the 1860s. She was the first person in the world to grow one. Today, the Granny Smith is grown all around the world.

## Tasks

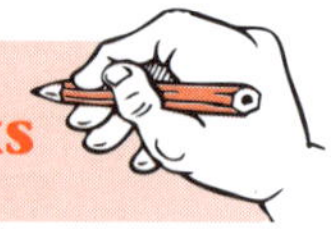

1. **Underline** the **adjective**.
2. **Highlight** the **word** that describes the shape of an apple.
3. **Circle** the words that **name** the different varieties of apple.
4. **Underline** a **fact** that states when apples are harvested.
5. **Highlight** the **proper nouns**.
6. **Circle** the **words** that tell where the Granny Smith is grown today.

# Student B: Monica's draft

Monica, another Year 3 student, is going to write an **information report** about bananas.

Look at her photos and notes.

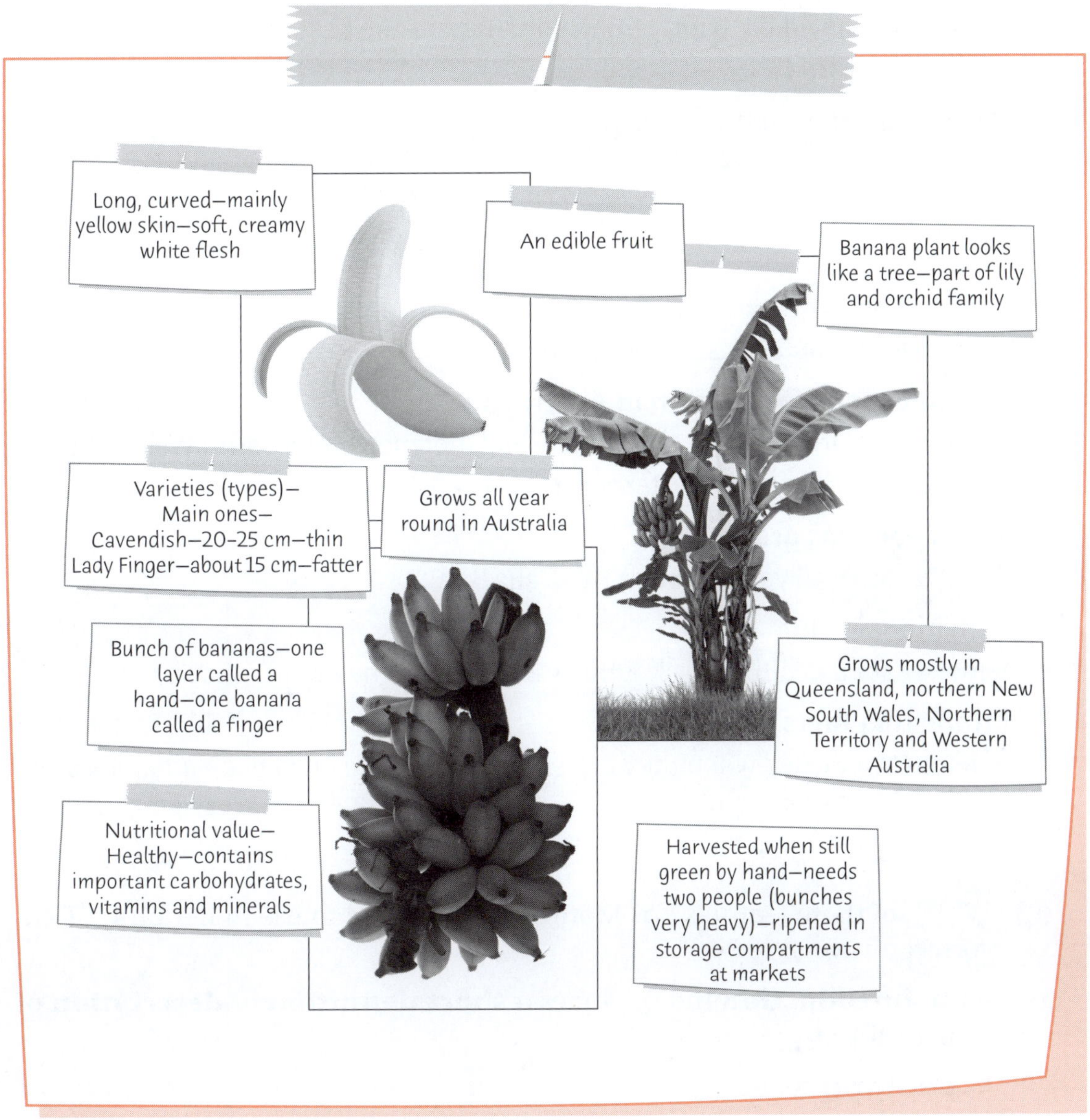


Help Monica fill in the answers.

1. List two **adjectives** that describe a banana's shape.

______________________________

2. What is a **group** of bananas called?

   For example: *A group of sheep is a* **flock**.

______________________________

# Writing the first draft

This is Monica's **first draft**. Read what she wrote and then answer the questions.

## Bananas

**Introduction**

A banana is an edible fruit. I think bananas are the best kind of fruit.

**Appearance**

Bananas are long and curved. They have mainly yellow skins. Their flesh is soft and a creamy white colour.

**Varieties**

There are two main varieties.

**How bananas grow**

Bananas grow on plants that look like trees.

**Where bananas are grown in Australia**

Bananas are grown mainly in Queensland, northern New South Wales, the Northern Territory and Western Australia.

**When bananas grow**

Bananas grow all year round in Australia.

**Nutritional value**

Bananas are a healthy snack. I think they are the healthiest snack.

**Interesting facts**

Bananas are picked when they are still green. It takes two people to pick one bunch of bananas.

1. Which of these features has Monica remembered to use in her draft? Tick (✓) the correct answers.

   a. an **introduction** that includes a **short definition** or **description** of her subject ☐

   b. **paragraphs** that give **information** about her subject ☐

   c. **subheadings** to organise her **paragraphs** ☐

   d. only **facts**, not opinions ☐

   e. **technical** or special **language** that refers specifically to bananas (e.g. *Cavendish, Lady Finger)* ☐

   f. **present-tense verbs** ☐

   g. **correct spelling** and **punctuation** ☐

   h. a **conclusion** that **rounds off** her report ☐

2. Find two **opinions** that Monica has expressed in her draft and underline them.

# Step-by-step improvement plan

Monica is also going to do some practice exercises to find ways to improve her **information report**. Help her complete them.

## Step 1: Start with a good introduction

This is what Monica has written in her introduction.

A banana is an edible fruit.
I think bananas are the best kind of fruit.

The second sentence is an **opinion**. Replace it with a sentence that tells what family of plants bananas belong to. Use Monica's notes to help you.

A banana is an edible fruit.
It is part of ____________

____________

____________

____________

## Step 2: Use technical language

**Technical language** is special language that is used to talk about a **particular** subject.

For example: *The words* **Red Delicious, Pink Lady** *and* **Fuji** *are special names for different types of* **apples**.

Using technical language when writing information reports shows that you have a good understanding of the subject.

1. Which **technical words** could Monica use to name the different varieties of banana?

   ____________

2. Use Monica's notes to help you complete the following sentences.

   **a** One layer of bananas in a bunch is called a ____________.

   **b** A single banana is called a ____________.

3. Write a sentence about bananas using these **technical terms**:

   *carbohydrates* *vitamins* *minerals*

   ____________

   ____________

   ____________

   ____________

## Step 3: Add detail to paragraphs

Use Monica's notes to help you complete the following sentences.

1. Bananas grow on tall plants that look like ______________________. The bananas grow in ______________________ on the trees.
2. Bananas are picked by hand when they are still green. It takes two people to pick one bunch of bananas because ________________________________________________

________________________________________________

The bananas are ripened ________________________________________________

________________________________________________

## Step 4: State facts, not opinions

Use these pictures to help you sort the **facts** from the **opinions** in the sentences below. Write F next to the facts, and O next to the opinions.

1. Bananas can be dried. ☐
2. Dried bananas are tastier than fresh bananas. ☐
3. The most delicious smoothies are the ones with bananas in them. ☐
4. Bananas are used with other fruits to make smoothies. ☐
5. Bananas with speckled skins taste horrible. ☐
6. Some bananas have speckled skins. ☐

# Writing the final draft

Monica has started writing the **final draft** of her **information report**. Help her complete it and then look in the answers section to compare what you have written with what she wrote.

**Hint!** Look at the practice exercises and Monica's notes for ideas.

## Bananas

**Introduction**

A banana is an edible fruit. It is part of the lily and orchid family.

**Appearance**

A banana is a long, curved fruit. It has a thick, yellow skin and soft, creamy white flesh. Bananas are between 15 and 25 cm long.

**Varieties**

There are two main varieties of banana, the ..............................

..............................

..............................

**How bananas grow**

Bananas grow in bunches on plants that look like trees. One layer of bananas in a bunch is called a hand, and a single banana is called a finger.

**Where bananas are grown**

In Australia, bananas are grown mainly in Queensland, northern New South Wales, the Northern Territory and Western Australia.

**When bananas are grown**

..............................

..............................

**Nutritional value**

Bananas are healthy to eat because they contain carbohydrates, vitamins and minerals.

**Interesting facts**

Bananas are picked by hand when ..............................

..............................

..............................

..............................

..............................

# Your turn

Write an **information report** of about a page on one of the following. Use your own paper for this activity.

**Writing Checklist** Make sure your information report includes: ✓

- an **introduction** that includes a **short description** of the subject. ☐
- a **detailed description** of the subject presented as a **series** of **paragraphs**. ☐
- **paragraphs** with **headings** that tell the reader what the paragraphs are about. ☐
- **facts**, not opinions. ☐
- **technical** or **special language**. ☐
- **present-tense verbs**. ☐
- **correct spelling** and **punctuation**. ☐
- a **conclusion** that **rounds off** the report. ☐

**Tip** Use **Rashid's final draft** on page 66 and **Monica's final draft** on page 71 to help you write your report.

Go to WORD BANK page 106 for useful vocabulary

1. What is your favourite fruit? Find out all you can about it and then write an information report about it.
2. Use the information below to write a report about the pumpkin.

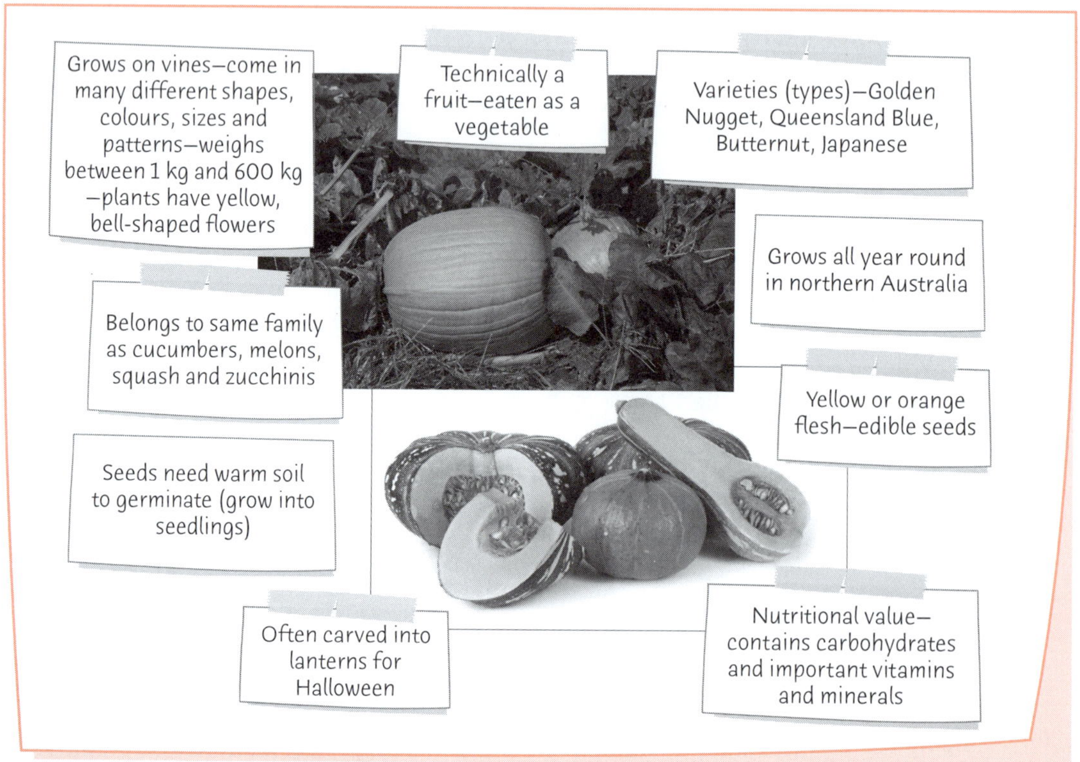

# Unit 7 Writing to give advice—holiday reviews

## Looking at reviews

A **review** is a report in which you give your personal opinion about something. You can review books, plays or even holidays.

In this unit we will be reviewing holidays.

A **holiday review** should have:

* an **introduction** that names the holiday place and tells your reader where it is.
* middle **paragraphs** that give more detail and opinions about what there is to see and do there.
* a **conclusion** that contains your personal opinion of the place and advice for visitors (e.g. what type of clothes to pack and the best time of year to visit).

**Hint!** Be careful not to simply write a recount of your visit. The following texts will help you tell the difference between a recount and a review.

**Recount** Last year my family and I went to Kiama. It took us about two hours to get there. We were there for a week. We went to the beach every day. Sometimes we played in the park. We also went snorkelling. I had a really good time. I would like to go there again.

**Review** Last year my family and I spent a week in Kiama. Kiama is a small town about two hours south of Sydney. The beaches are great, and there is a beautiful park where people can have picnics. I think Kiama is the perfect place for a family holiday.

Now look at the following texts. Which one is the **review**? Tick (✓) the correct answer.

**A** Last October my family and I went to Brisbane. Brisbane is the capital city of Queensland. One of the best places to visit in Brisbane is South Bank. The pools and parks are great for children to play in. I would definitely visit Brisbane again. ☐

**B** Last October my family and I went to Brisbane. We went by aeroplane. That was exciting! We stayed in a hotel. My favourite place was South Bank. We went there every day. We also went on a ferry. I enjoyed my visit to Brisbane. ☐

# Student A: Larissa's draft

Larissa's Year 3 class are adding a travel advice section to their website. Each student is going to write a **review** of a place they have visited to post on the website.

Larissa is going to write a review of Kakadu National Park.

First, she jotted down some notes about her visit in her journal.

## Holiday Review

**Where**: Kakadu National Park—Northern Territory—171 km south-east of Darwin

**When**: Last year in July

**Things to do**: Go to Warradjan Aboriginal Cultural Centre
Go on cruise on Yellow Waters Wetland
Go on walking trails

**Things to see**: Aboriginal arts and crafts, rock art, birds, crocodiles, huge termite mounds, wild brumbies

**What I learnt**: Bininj people traditional owners of land—have lived in Kakadu for more than 50 000 years

**My opinions of Kakadu**: Liked it—guides knew a lot—didn't like all the flies and mosquitoes!

**Rating**: ★★★★★

1. List five **proper nouns** that Larissa has used to name places. Remember: proper nouns name people, places and things and always start with a capital letter.

2. Write the **proper noun** that names a group of people.

3. Larissa took this photograph in Kakadu National Park. What do you think it shows? Use Larissa's notes to help you find the answer.

# Writing the first draft

This is the **first draft** of Larissa's **review**. Read what she has written and then answer the questions.

> ## Kakadu National Park
>
> ★★★★★
>
> Last year I went to Kakadu National Park. There are lots of things to see and do there.
>
> One of the things you can do in Kakadu is go to the Warradjan Aboriginal Cultural Centre.
>
> You can also go on a cruise on the Yellow Waters Wetland. You will see birds and crocodiles.
>
> You can go on walking trails. You will see Aboriginal rock art, huge termite mounds and wild brumbies.
>
> I liked lots of things about Kakadu. I didn't like all the flies and mosquitoes.

1. A good **review** of a holiday place should contain the following features. Tick (✓) the ones that Larissa has used.
   - **a** an **introduction** that names the place and also tells where it is ☐
   - **b** a **middle section** that contains more **detail** and **opinions** about what there is to see and do there ☐
   - **c** **adjectives that express opinions** (e.g. *an* **adventurous** *holiday*) ☐
   - **d** **correct spelling** and **punctuation** ☐
   - **e** a **conclusion** that contains **personal opinions** about the place and **advice** for visitors ☐

2. Larissa has correctly used present-, past- and future-tense verbs in her draft. In which tense are the underlined **verbs** in the following sentences?
   - **a** There <u>are</u> lots of things to see and do there. ____________
   - **b** You <u>will see</u> birds and crocodiles. ____________
   - **c** I <u>liked</u> lots of things about Kakadu. ____________

3. What is a brumby? Tick (✓) the correct answer.

| wild pig ☐ | wild bull ☐ | wild horse ☐ |
|---|---|---|

# Step-by-step improvement plan

Larissa wants to improve her **review**. She is going to do some exercises to find ways to do this. Help her complete them.

## Step 1: Start with a good introduction

The **introduction** is the opening paragraph. It should tell your reader **where** the place is and **when** you went there. This information will help your readers decide if they want to visit the place.

Help Larissa write a better **introduction** by filling in the following information. Use her notes to help you.

Last (name the month) ______________ I went to Kakadu National Park with my family.

The park is in (name the state or territory) ________________________________________.

It is about (say how far it is from a big town or city) ________________________________

____________________________________________________________________________

## Step 2: Add detail to paragraphs

In Unit 6 you learnt that a **paragraph** is a **group of sentences** about one thing. Adding **detail** to paragraphs makes your writing more interesting to read.

Help Larissa add the following information to her second **paragraph**.

Warradjan—
Aboriginal name—
means pig-nosed turtle

a round building—
looks like turtle

interesting
information about
Aboriginal culture

One of the things you can do in Kakadu is go to the Warradjan Aboriginal Cultural Centre.

Warradjan is _______________________________________________________________

____________________________________________________________________________.

The building is _____________________________________________________________

____________________________________________________________________________.

It has _____________________________________________________________________

____________________________________________________________________________.

## Step 3: Use adjectives to express opinions

**Adjectives** add meaning to nouns. They can help us express opinions or points of view (e.g. *It was a* **good** *holiday*).

**1** Choose an **adjective** from the box to complete each of the following sentences. Use each adjective once.

| | | | | |
|---|---|---|---|---|
| *exciting* | *adventurous* | *good* | *wonderful* | *interesting* |

**a** Visiting Kakadu is a ______________________ experience.

**b** If you want an ______________________ holiday, you should definitely think of visiting Kakadu.

**c** There is lots of ______________________ information in the Warradjan Aboriginal Cultural Centre.

**d** Kakadu is an ______________________ place to visit.

**e** The guides are very ______________________ and know a lot about the park.

**2** Complete the **phrases** beneath each of these photos Larissa took in Kakadu National Park (e.g. *a spectacular* **sunset**).

**a** a stunning ______________________

**b** a peaceful ______________________

**c** beautiful ______________________

**d** a magnificent ______________________

**3** Use the **adjective** *amazing* to write an opinion of a place you have visited.

______________________________________________

______________________________________________

# Writing the final draft

This is Larissa's **final draft**. Read the comments about her **review** on the left, and do the tasks on the right.

**Comments**

**Tasks**

## Kakadu National Park

★★★★★

*A good* ***introduction*** *gives the name of the place and tells where it is.*

Last July I visited Kakadu National Park with my family. The park is in the Northern Territory, about 171 km south-east of Darwin.

**1. Underline** the **sentence** that tells where Kakadu is.

*Using* ***paragraphs*** *helps to organise information.*

There are lots of interesting things to see and do in Kakadu, but visiting the Warradjan Aboriginal Cultural Centre is top of my list. Warradjan is an Aboriginal name for the pig-nosed turtle. The building is round, just like the turtle. Inside are displays of Aboriginal art and crafts. There is also lots of interesting information about how Aboriginals lived and how they used and cared for the land. I discovered that Aboriginals have lived in Kakadu for more than 50 000 years, and that the Bininj people are the traditional owners of the land.

**2. Highlight** the **adjective** that expresses an opinion about the information in the centre.

*Using* ***adjectives*** *helps the writer express opinions about the place.*

Another highlight for me was cruising through the Yellow Waters Wetland. We took the sunrise cruise and saw some brilliant birds and quite a few crocodiles. Our guide was very good and knew a lot about the park.

**3. Circle** the **adjective** that expresses an opinion about the guide.

Some of the other exciting things we saw were Aboriginal rock art, huge termite mounds and wild brumbies.

**4. Underline** the **adjective** that describes the termite mounds.

*Giving your readers* ***advice*** *helps to wrap up the review.*

If you want an adventurous holiday, you should definitely think of visiting Kakadu. Just take lots of insect repellent to keep the flies and mosquitoes away!

**5. Highlight** the reviewer's final piece of **advice** to the readers.

## Student B: Theo's draft

Theo, another Year 3 student, is going to write a **review** of the Jenolan Caves.

### Holiday Review

**Where**: Jenolan Caves—in Blue Mountains World Heritage area—New South Wales— about 180 km west of Sydney

**When**: Last school holidays

**About the caves**: 10 caves open to public—visited Lucas, Imperial and Chifley Caves—millions of years old—bones of Ice Age animals buried deep inside—Lucas the biggest cave—huge chambers—Cathedral used for musical performances

**My opinion of the caves**: Enjoyed it

**Advice to visitors**: Wear sturdy shoes—take a jumper or jacket

**Rating**: ★★★★★

1. Why do you think Theo would advise visitors to wear sturdy shoes?

_______________

_______________

_______________

_______________

_______________

2. Why do you think he would advise visitors to take a jumper or jacket?

_______________

_______________

_______________

_______________

_______________

3. Use this photo Theo took inside the caves to help you complete the **sentence**.

Inside the caves, Theo saw stalactites and

_______________.

# Writing the first draft

This is the **first draft** of Theo's **review**. Read it and then answer the questions.

### The Jenolan Caves

★ ★ ★ ★ ★

In the last school holidays I went to the Jenolan Caves. I went with my family.

Ten caves are open to the public. We couldn't see them all. We took the tour through the Lucas, Imperial and Chifley Caves. The Lucas Cave has huge chambers. The biggest chamber is The Cathedral. It is 54 m high. It often is used for musical performances.

I really liked the Jenolan Caves. I'm glad I wore sturdy shoes and a jacket. It was cool inside the caves.

1. Which of these features has Theo remembered to include in his draft? Tick (✓) the correct answers.
   - a an **introduction** that names the place and tells where it is ☐
   - b a **middle section** that contains more detail and opinions about what there is to see and do there ☐
   - c **adjectives** that express **opinions** ☐
   - d **correct spelling** and **punctuation** ☐
   - e a **conclusion** that contains **personal opinions** of the place and **advice** for visitors ☐

2. Circle the following **verbs** in the draft:
   - a the present tense of *were* and *was used.*
   - b the past tense of *go, cannot, take* and *wear.*

3. Write the **adjective** that Theo has used to describe:
   - a the chambers. ______________________
   - b his shoes. ______________________
   - c what it was like inside the caves. ______________________

# Step-by-step improvement plan

Theo is also going to do some exercises to find ways to improve his **review**. Help him complete them.

## Step 1: Start with a good introduction

Help Theo write a better **opening paragraph** by telling exactly where the Jenolan Caves are and how far they are from Sydney. Use his notes to help you.

**Where?** Jenolan Caves—in Blue Mountains World Heritage area—New South Wales—about 180 km west of Sydney

The Jenolan Caves are in ______________________________

______________________________

______________________________

______________________________

## Step 2: Use paragraphs to organise information

Remember: a **paragraph** is a group of sentences about one thing.

Using paragraphs helps you organise your information. It also makes your text easier to read.

Use Theo's notes to help you fill in the missing **paragraph**.

**About the caves**: 10 caves open to public—visited Lucas, Imperial and Chifley Caves—millions of years old—bones of Ice Age animals buried deep inside—Lucas the biggest cave—huge chambers—Cathedral used for musical performances—54 m high

**Paragraph 1**

Ten caves are open to the public. We couldn't see them all. We took the tour through the Lucas, Imperial and Chifley Caves.

**Paragraph 2**

______________________________

______________________________

______________________________

______________________________

______________________________

______________________________

**Paragraph 3**

The Lucas Cave is the biggest cave. It has huge chambers. The biggest chamber is The Cathedral. It is 54 m high. It is often used for musical performances.

## Step 3: Use adjectives to express opinions

1. Choose better **adjectives** from the box to replace the ones in bold. Use each adjective once.

| magnificent | magical | amazing |
| --- | --- | --- |

a I visited this **great** place with my family during the last school holidays. ____________

b The stalactites and stalagmites in the caves are a **great** sight. ____________

c A visit to the Jenolan Caves is a **great** experience. ____________

2. Complete the phrases beneath these photos that Theo took on his visit to the Jenolan Caves (e.g. *brilliant* **views**).

a unbelievable ____________

b fantastic ____________

c unusual ____________

d lovely ____________

3. Write a sentence about something you have seen that is spectacular. Make sure you use the **adjective** *spectacular* in your sentence.

____________

____________

# Writing the final draft

Theo has started writing the **final draft** of his **review**. Help him complete it, and then look in the answers section to compare what you have written with what Theo wrote.

**Hint!** Look at Theo's notes and the practice exercises to complete this exercise.

## The Jenolan Caves

★★★★★

I visited the Jenolan Caves with my family in the school holidays. These amazing caves are in the Blue Mountains World Heritage area in New South Wales. They are about 180 km west of Sydney.

There are ten caves that are open to the public, so we couldn't see them all. We took the tour through the Lucas, Imperial and Chifley Caves. The stalactites and stalagmites in the caves are a magnificent sight.

**(Tell about the guide and what she told you about the caves' age and the bones of Ice Age animals.)**

........................................................................................................................

........................................................................................................................

........................................................................................................................

........................................................................................................................

........................................................................................................................

........................................................................................................................

The Lucas Cave has the largest chambers. The biggest chamber, The Cathedral, is 54 m high. It is often used for musical performances because of its brilliant acoustics.

Visiting the Jenolan Caves is a magical experience. If you live in Sydney, you can easily go there for the day. **(Complete this paragraph with some advice for visitors.)**

........................................................................................................................

........................................................................................................................

........................................................................................................................

........................................................................................................................

........................................................................................................................

........................................................................................................................

........................................................................................................................

## Your turn

Write a **review** of one of the following. Use your own paper for this activity.

**Writing Checklist** Make sure your review includes: ✓

- an **introduction** that names the place and tells where it is. ☐
- **paragraphs** that contain more **detail** and **opinions** about what there is to see and do at the place. ☐
- **adjectives** that express **opinions**. ☐
- **correct spelling** and **punctuation**. ☐
- a **conclusion** that contains **personal opinions** of the place and **advice** for people who want to go there. ☐

**Tip** Use **Larissa's final draft** on page 78 and **Theo's final draft** on page 83 to help you write your review.

Go to WORD BANK page 106 for useful vocabulary

1. Write a review of a place that you have visited. It can be a place that you went to for a holiday or a place that you visited for the day.
2. Imagine you have been to Uluru for a holiday. Use the following information to write a review of your visit.

**Hint!** You do not need to use every bit of information.

**Where**: Uluru—in the Northern Territory—the red centre of Australia—about 450 km south-west of Alice Springs

**When**: last July

**About Uluru**: important to the Aboriginal people—348 m high—a sandstone formation—about 500 million years old

**Things to see and do**: watch the colours change on the rock at sunrise and sunset—ride camels—go on guided walks—learn about Aboriginal culture—have dinner under the stars—go to Uluru-Kata Tjuta National Park —see the rock formations

**My opinion of Uluru**: an unforgettable holiday, amazing sights, spectacular colours and rock formations

**Advice to visitors**: go in the winter—not so hot, not so many flies—take sunglasses, hat and something warm to wear at night

**Rating**: ★★★★★

# Unit 8 Explaining how a simple machine works

## Looking at explanations

An **explanation** tells us **why** something happens or **how** it works.

An explanation should have:

- an **opening statement** that introduces your topic.
  For example: *Telescopes are made up of many different parts that make distant objects appear closer.*
- **paragraphs** that explain how something works or why something happens.
- a **conclusion** that either sums up the explanation or ties it up in some other way.

**Hint!** We often add diagrams to explanations.

Read the following paragraph that explains how a telescope works and then answer the questions.

> First, the big end of the telescope gathers light from the object you're looking at. The lens at the big end makes a small, bright image. Then, the small lens in the eyepiece magnifies the image so that it appears much closer.

1. In which tense have the underlined **verbs** been written?

   past ☐ present ☐ future ☐

2. Circle two **time connectives** in the explanation. (Remember: time connectives show the order in which things happen.)

3. Highlight the word that means *makes bigger*.

4. Circle the **nouns** in the following list:

   telescope big lens eyepiece closer

# Student A: Li's draft

Li's Year 3 class are learning about simple machines, like levers, wedges, pulleys and screws. They each have to choose one simple machine and write an **explanation** of how it works. Li is going to explain how a simple lever works.

First, Li looked at diagrams of different levers.

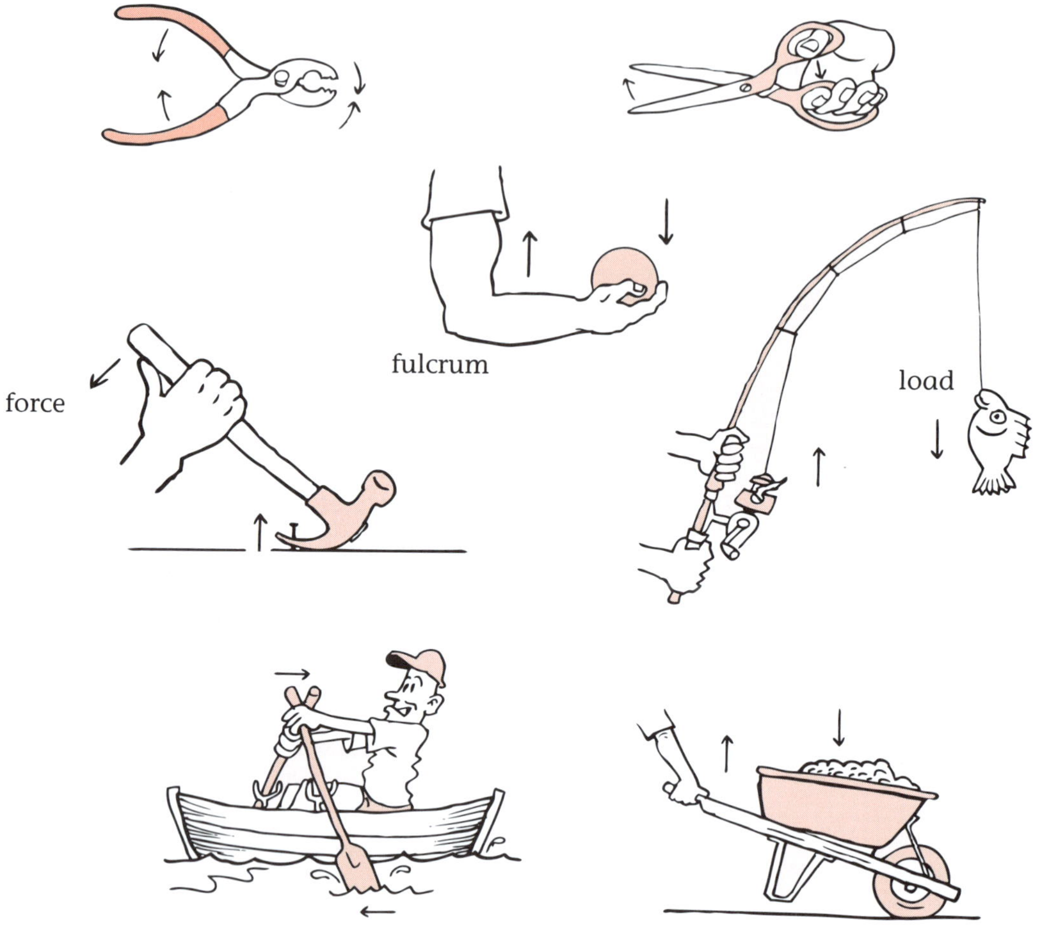


1. Use the words below to label the diagrams.

arm   hammer   scissors   fishing rod   oars   wheelbarrow   pliers

2. Which is the only **plural noun** in the list above? ______________________

**Hint!** It's the one where there are two of them.

3. Use the diagrams to help you complete the following:

Bat is to ball as

**a** nail is to ____________________   **b** boat is to ____________________

**c** hand is to ____________________   **d** hook is to ____________________

# Writing the first draft

This is Li's **first draft**. Read what he wrote and then answer the questions.

## How a Simple Lever Works

Levers are simple machines. They make it easier for us to push or pull things.

A seesaw is a lever. It has a board that sits on something. This is how it works.

Someone pushed on one end of the board. They moved down. The person on the other end moved up.

Levers are very useful machines. We use them every day.

1. A good **explanation** should contain the following features. Tick (✓) the ones Li has used.
   - **a** an **opening statement** that introduces the topic ☐
   - **b** **paragraphs** that explain **how** something works or **why** something happens ☐
   - **c** **present-tense verbs** throughout (e.g. *is, has* or *pushes*) ☐
   - **d** **technical** or **special language** to talk about the subject (e.g. *force* or *fulcrum*) ☐
   - **e** **correct spelling** and **punctuation** ☐
   - **f** a **conclusion** that either **sums up** the **explanation** or **ties it up** in some other way ☐

2. Explanations should contain only present-tense verbs. Underline two **verbs** that Li has incorrectly written in the **past tense**.

# Step-by-step improvement plan

Li is going to do some exercises to find ways to improve his **explanation**. Help him complete them.

## Step 1: Start with a good opening statement

The **opening statement** is the first paragraph of your explanation. It should give your reader a general description of a lever by telling what **it is** and what **it does**.

Which of these **sentences** best describes a lever and what it does?

1. There are lots of levers in our house and garage. ☐
2. A lever is a simple machine that makes work easier. ☐
3. A lever is a useful machine. ☐

## Step 2: Use technical language

Machines like levers have their own words to name the different parts and processes.
For example: *keyboard, mouse* and *monitor* are technical words that refer to parts of a computer.

Using **technical language** in an explanation shows that you have a good knowledge of the subject.

Replace the underlined words in the following sentences with a **technical word** from the list. Use the diagrams on page 86 to help you.

fulcrum    load    force

1. A lever works by placing a stiff board or rod on a point. ____________
2. Someone applies a push ____________ to one end of the board or rod.
3. This moves the thing ____________ at the other end in the opposite direction.

## Step 3: Use present-tense verbs

A **verb** is the most important word in a sentence. It tells us what someone or something is **doing**.
For example: *We* **use** *the machine.*

Sometimes it does not express an action.
For example: *A lever* **is** *a simple machine. A wheelbarrow* **has** *two handles.*

**Tense** tells us when something **happens**: in the present (e.g. *use*), in the past (e.g. *used*) or in the future (e.g. *will use*).

We use **present tense** in explanations to show that the action always happens this way (e.g. *it moves up*), not only once (e.g. *it moved up*).

Change the underlined verbs in these sentences so that they are in the **present tense**.

1. The board or rod turned ________________ on the fulcrum.
2. A seesaw was __________ a good example of how a lever worked ______________.
3. Someone applied ________________ force to one end of the board.
4. The load on the other end of the board moved ________________ in the opposite direction.
5. Levers were ________________ very useful machines.

## Step 4: Wrap up the explanation with a good conclusion.

The **conclusion** is the final paragraph of your explanation. It should **tie it up** in an interesting way.

The following paragraph would make a good **conclusion** for Li's explanation. Complete it by filling in words from the box.

| | | | | |
|---|---|---|---|---|
| useful | simple | levers | wheels | combined |

People have been using ________________ for centuries. They are very ________________ machines, especially when they are ________________ with other ________________ machines like wedges and ________________.

# Writing the final draft

This is Li's **final draft**. Read the comments about his **explanation** on the left, and do the tasks on the right.

**Comments**

*The* ***opening statement*** *gives a general introduction to the topic.*

*Using* ***technical language*** *shows that the writer has a good knowledge of the subject.*

*Adding a* ***diagram*** *helps the reader understand how the machine works.*

*Using* ***present-tense verbs*** *shows that the actions can be done at any time.*

*Ending with an interesting* ***conclusion*** *wraps up the explanation.*

## How a Simple Lever Works

A lever is a simple machine that makes work easier.

Any object that has a handle acts as a lever. Tools such as scissors, staplers, pliers and wheelbarrows all work as levers.

Levers work by placing a bar or rod on a point, called a fulcrum. The board or rod turns on this point. A seesaw is a good example of how a lever works.

First, someone applies force to one end of the board by pushing on it. The person on the other end of the board then moves in the opposite direction. The person or object that the lever moves is called the load.

People have been using levers for centuries. They are very useful machines, especially when they are combined with other simple machines like wedges and wheels.

**Tasks**

1. **Underline** the **words** that tell what a lever does.
2. **Highlight** the **list** of items.
3. **Circle** the **technical word**.
4. **Underline** two **connectives**.
5. **Highlight** the **words** that tell how long people have been using levers.

## Student B: Charlotte's draft

Charlotte, another Year 3 student, is going to write an **explanation** of how a simple pulley works.

She starts by studying some diagrams of simple pulleys

1

2

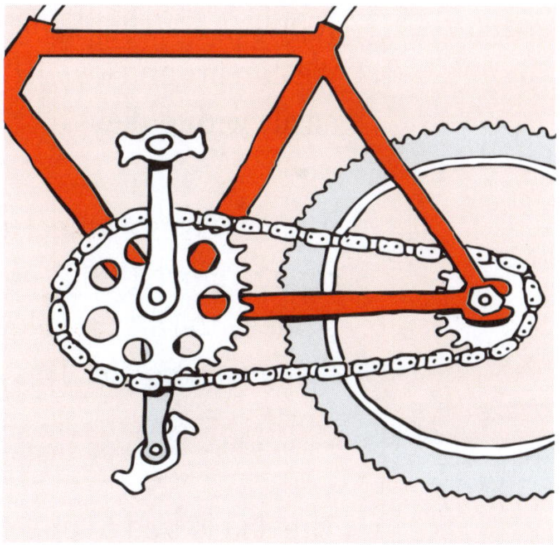

3

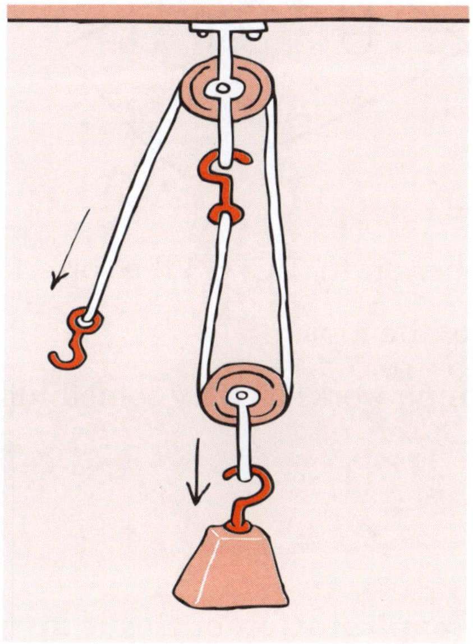

4

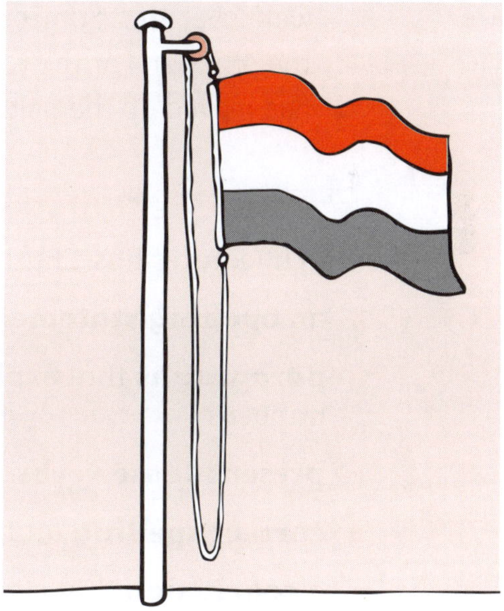

1. Which two pulleys pictured above are you likely to see at a school?

_______________________________________________

2. Fill in the following labels on picture number 1: Force Load

3. Complete the following sentence:

   A bicycle moves forward when the rider applies force by ______________________

   _______________________________________________

## Writing the first draft

This is Charlotte's **first draft**. Read what she wrote and then answer the questions.

### How a Simple Pulley Works

A pulley is a simple machine. We can lift and lower things easily with pulleys.

A pulley uses a wheel and a rope to move things. We use a pulley to raise and lower a flag on a flagpole. This is how it works.

The flag is tied to one end of the rope. There was a wheel at the top of the pole. The rope went over this. Someone pulled the other end of the rope. The flag moved up the pole.

1. Which features has Charlotte included in her draft? Tick (✓) the correct answers.
   - a an **opening statement** that introduces the topic ☐
   - b **paragraphs** that explain **how** something works or **why** something happens ☐
   - c **present-tense verbs** throughout ☐
   - d **correct spelling** and **punctuation** ☐
   - e a **conclusion** that either **sums up** the **explanation** or **ties it up** in some other way ☐
2. Charlotte has incorrectly used past-tense **verbs** in the last four sentences. Find them and underline them.
3. In the text, find and underline these words.
   - a the opposite of *raise* ______________________
   - b a word that means *fastened* ______________________
   - c the opposite of *pushed* ______________________

# Step-by-step improvement plan

Charlotte is also going to do some practice exercises to find ways to improve her **explanation**. Help her complete them.

## Step 1: Start with a good introduction

This is how Charlotte started her explanation.

A pulley is a simple machine. We can lift and lower things easily with pulleys.

Help Charlotte make her two sentences into one long **sentence**.

A pulley is a ______________________________

______________________________

______________________________

______________________________

## Step 2: Use present-tense verbs

1 Rewrite the following words in the **present tense**.

| | | | |
|---|---|---|---|
| built | ________ | worked | ________ |
| lifted | ________ | fastened | ________ |
| made | ________ | started | ________ |
| used | ________ | raised | ________ |

2 In the following sentences, circle the **present-tense verb** inside the brackets.

a Examples of simple machines (were, are) pulleys, levers and wedges.

b A rope (is, was) passed through a wheel at the top of the flagpole.

c Someone (pulls, pulled) on the other side of the rope.

d The rope (moved, moves) up the flagpole.

e Some very big pulleys (have, has) more than one wheel.

f These big pulleys (could, can) move very heavy loads.

## Step 3: End with an interesting conclusion

Use three of the sentences below to write a good **conclusion** for Charlotte's explanation. Your paragraph must make sense.

For example: you wouldn't write *They use steel cables instead of ropes. Cranes have more than one wheel. A crane is a very big pulley.*

**Hint!** Start with either a or c.

a A crane is a very big pulley.

b They use steel cables instead of ropes.

c Some very big pulleys, like cranes, have more than one wheel.

d Cranes have more than one wheel.

e These big pulleys can move very heavy loads.

# Writing the final draft

Charlotte has started writing the **final draft** of her **explanation**. Help her complete it, and then look in the answers section to compare what you have written with what Charlotte wrote.

**Hint!** Look at the diagrams and the practice exercises for ideas.

## How a Simple Pulley Works

A pulley is a simple machine that uses a wheel and a rope to lift, lower or move a load.

A flagpole is a good example of a simple pulley. **(Explain how a flag is raised on a flagpole.)**

Some very big pulleys, like cranes, have more than one wheel. They use steel cables instead of ropes. These big pulleys can move very heavy loads.

# Your turn

Write an **explanation** of about a page on one of the following. Use your own paper for this activity.

**Writing Checklist** Make sure your explanation contains: ✓

- an **opening statement** that gives a **general introduction** to the topic. ☐
- **paragraphs** that explain **how** the object or process works or **why** it happens. ☐
- **present-tense verbs** throughout. ☐
- **technical words** if necessary. ☐
- **correct spelling** and **punctuation**. ☐
- a **conclusion** that either **sums up** the **explanation** or **ties it up** in some other way. ☐

**Tip** Use **Li's final draft** on page 90 and **Charlotte's final draft** on page 95 to help you write your explanation.

Go to WORD BANK page 106 for useful vocabulary

Write an explanation that describes how one of these simple machines works.

1. a simple wedge

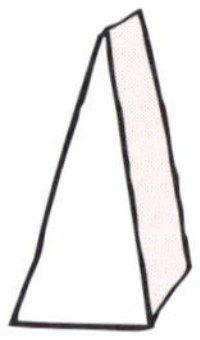

2. a simple wheel and axle

3. a simple inclined plane

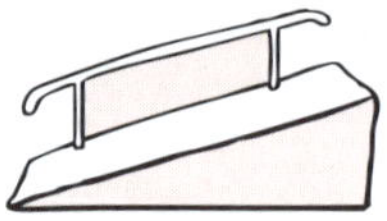

4. a simple screw

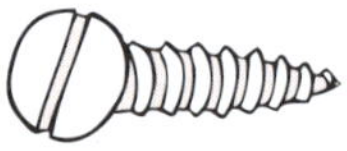

# Answers

## Unit 1 Writing a recount

### Page 1

1 a Yesterday b at Ben's house
c The writer, Ben, Ben's mum and Ben's puppy
d went, played, kicked, stopped, called, finished, was, had
e Ben and I had a great time!

2 b, d and e

### Page 2

1 1 b 2 a 3 d 4 c

2 Jessica and Annie brought me presents. Annie gave me a book. Everybody sang 'Happy birthday' to me. I blew out the candles.

### Page 3

1 a, b, d, e, f

2 a in December b at my house

3 a brought b got c sang
d blew e went

4 Choose three of these: turned, had, came, gave, played

### Pages 4–5

**Step 1**

1 a at 2.30 pm b at the door
c straight away d around the table
e with a single breath f in the garden
g at five o'clock

2 WHEN: at five o'clock
WHERE: in the garden
HOW: with a single breath

**Step 2**

1 At last 2 After that/Afterwards
3 Meanwhile 4 then
5 Afterwards/After that 6 Finally

**Step 3**

1 B

2 Suggested answer: My friends gave me exactly what I wanted!

### Page 6

1 at our house 2 was, couldn't, gave
3 After that

4 a with balloons and streamers
b with a single breath

5 Afterwards

6 That was definitely the best birthday party I've ever had!

### Page 7

1 1 d 2 c 3 a 4 b

2 Suggested answers:
a We had a great time watching the seal show.
b We discussed what we had seen while eating lunch.
c We saw some wonderful sights at the bird show.
d Everyone was laughing at the chimps.

### Page 8

1 b, d, e, f, g

2 a went b was c laughed

3 I really enjoyed seeing all the animals!

### Pages 9–10

**Step 1**

A

**Step 2**

1 at the zoo 2 around the enclosure
3 at feeding time 4 above my head
5 from the shop 6 under a shady tree
7 with a treat

**Step 3**

1 First 2 Then/Next 3 Afterwards
4 Before 5 After lunch 6 Then/Next
7 Last of all

### Page 11

**Our Visit to the Zoo**

Just after we got back to school this year, Mrs Gonzalez gave us the exciting news—we were going on an excursion to the zoo to learn more about endangered animals.

We travelled to the zoo by bus. When we arrived there, we were divided into groups. I was in Mrs Gonzalez's group.

First we went to see the chimps. Three small chimpanzees were chasing each other around the enclosure. They were so funny!

Afterwards we made our way to the giraffes' enclosure. We were lucky to get there at feeding time. One of the giraffes wouldn't come out of the shelter. We could just see its head looking out above the wooden gate.

Next, Mrs Gonzalez took us to see the reptiles and the rainforest. I thought that some of the reptiles looked scary, especially the enormous grey crocodile, but the rainforest was cool and relaxing and I enjoyed looking at the colourful birds.

Before the bird show started, there was just enough time to have something to eat. We found a good spot under a shady tree to sit and have our lunch.

After lunch we went to the bird show. It was brilliant! I couldn't believe how clever those birds were! One of them hovered right above my head. I thought it was going to use me as a perch!

Then we listened to a talk on endangered animals. It was very interesting, and we even got to hold a couple of the rainforest animals. It was the first time I'd ever touched a snake. I thought it would feel slimy, but its skin was dry.

Last of all we watched the seal show. The seals performed some amazing tricks and their trainer rewarded them with a treat.

I was exhausted when we finally got onto the bus to come back to school, but I'd had a great time looking at all the animals.

## Unit 2 Writing a procedure

### Page 13

1 This is how you make a paper aeroplane.
2 a sheet of A4 paper
3 First, Next, Then, After that, Finally
4 fold

### Page 14

### Page 15

1 **b**, **g**
2 wholemeal bread, butter, cooked chicken, tomato, cucumber, lettuce leaves, sprouts, carrot, beetroot, mayonnaise
chopping board, large nylon knife, small nylon knife, tongs, grater, small plate
3 Cut two slices of bread and spread some butter on them. Cut the chicken into shreds. Cut the tomato and cucumber into slices.
4 **a** over the lettuce leaves
**b** into two triangles

### Pages 16–17

**Step 1**

1 How to Make a Chicken Salad Sandwich
2 This is what you need to make a chicken salad sandwich.

**Step 2**

Suggested answers:
1 Grate the carrot.
2 Put the chicken on the bread.
3 Put mayonnaise over the lettuce leaves.
4 Cover it with the other slice.
5 Serve it on a plate.

**Step 3**

Step 1 **c** Step 2 **b** Step 3 **e** Step 4 **a** Step 5 **d**

**Step 4**

1 Pull 2 Squirt

### Page 18

1 wholemeal bread, butter, cooked chicken, tomato, cucumber, lettuce leaves, sprouts, carrot, beetroot, mayonnaise
2 large, nylon, small
3 First
4 pull, grate, Slice
5 tomato, cucumber, sprouts and carrot
6 place
7 After that
8 cut, serve

### Page 19

1

2

## Page 20

1 b, c, g

2 a squeeze b ask c cut
d add e mix f dish

3 a large, small, big b healthy

## Pages 21–22

**Step 1**

1 How to Make a Fruit Salad

2 This is how you make a fruit salad.

**Step 2**

Suggested answers:

1 Peel the banana.

2 Squeeze lemon over the fruit.

3 Chop the pineapple.

4 Mix the fruit together.

**Step 3**

1 First 2 Then/Next/After that

3 Then/Next/After that 4 Then/Next/After that

5 Finally

**Step 4**

1 ripe 2 crunchy

3 seedless 4 juicy

## Page 23

**How to Make a Fruit Salad**

This is how you make a fruit salad.

**Ingredients:** watermelon, papaya, rockmelon, pineapple, apple, banana, mango, lemon

**Utensils:** chopping board, large nylon knife, small nylon knife, large bowl, small bowl, large spoon

**Steps:**

First, peel the banana and chop the apple.

Then, put the fruit in the big bowl and squeeze lemon juice over it. This stops it from turning brown.

Cut the rest of the fruit into chunks and add it to the bowl.

Finally, mix the fruit together with a large spoon.

Serve in a small bowl.

# Unit 3 Describing a person

## Page 25

1 a narrative b information report

2 a The tall man arrived in a silver car.
b The sun shone brightly on the still water.

## Page 26

1 curly, brown, twinkly, blue, few, pink, short, plump, kind, excellent

2 cooking and gardening

## Page 27

1 c, d, f

2 a has b is c enjoys

3 delicious, tasty, scrumptious, heavenly

## Pages 28–29

**Step 1**

I call my grandmother Gran. She calls herself an eco warrior. That means she fights to save the environment. It makes her sound fierce but she's really very sweet and kind.

**Step 2**

1 and 2 so 3 because 4 but

5 or 6 while 7 unless

**Step 3**

I also admire her for the wonderful work she does for the environment. Gran is definitely one of my favourite people!

## Page 30

1 fierce, sweet, kind 2 so 3 most amazing

4 fit, healthy 5 but

6 Gran is definitely one of my favourite people!

## Page 31

1 a tall, thin, straight, black
b stylish, clever, patient, popular

2 play basketball and go to the gym

## Page 32

1 c, d, f

2 a goes, is going, am going b has

3 studious

## Pages 33–34

**Step 1**

Suggested answer:

Many of my friends complain about their older brothers and sisters, but I'm lucky. I have a great older brother.

### Step 2

Suggested answers:

1 a Malik is tall and thin and has straight black hair.

b Malik is studying to be a doctor so he is still at university.

c Malik is very fit because he goes to the gym every day.

d Malik is very clever but he also works very hard.

e Malik will stay at home with us until he finishes university.

2 a Although b when c unless

### Step 3

I admire my brother because he is so kind and smart. I work hard at school so that one day I will also be able to go to university and become a doctor like Malik. He is my hero!

## Page 35

**My Brother**

Many of my friends complain about their older brothers and sisters, but I am lucky. I have a great older brother.

My brother's name is Malik. He is twenty years old. He is tall and thin and has straight black hair. He wears very stylish clothes and always looks smart. He goes to the gym every day so he is very fit.

Malik is studying to be a doctor, so he is still at university. He is very clever but he also works hard. I think he will be a very good doctor because he is so kind and patient.

Although Malik has lots of university work to do, he still has time to play basketball. He is very good at it. He is also very popular and has lots of friends.

I admire my brother because he is so smart and kind. I work hard at school so that one day I will also be able to go to university and become a doctor like Malik. He is my hero!

# Unit 4 Writing to persuade—expositions

## Page 37

1 b 2 b

## Page 38

1 excellent teachers—interesting lessons, kind and helpful, take us on excursions, kind and caring principal

2 cool playground—amazing playground equipment, shady trees, basketball court

3 great library—lots of books, magazines and newspapers, the heart of the school

## Page 39

1 a, b, d, f, g

2 a interesting b shady c amazing

3 That is

## Pages 40–41

### Step 1

1 like/love, know 2 hope 3 thinks

4 decided 5 love/like

### Step 2

Firstly, also, Secondly, In addition, Finally, so

### Step 3

1 B

2 b

3 Suggestion: Now that you know what a great school North Park Public is, I am sure you will all want to come here next year.

## Page 42

1 I think you should come to North Park Public School

2 always ready to help us, take us on excursions, For example, we visited the zoo to learn how we can help save endangered animals.

3 Secondly, so

4 In addition, also

5 It is packed with books, magazines and newspapers.

6 sure

## Page 43

1 lots of shops 2 good public transport system

3 lots of places to have fun and relax

## Pages 44–45

1 a, b, d, f, g

2 a excited b good c regular

3 you're, It's

4 a There's b You'll

## Pages 45–46

### Step 1

1 believe/think 2 suppose, think/believe

3 wonder, know 4 imagine 5 enjoy

### Step 2

1 a as well as b also c such as

d for example e In addition

2 Suggestions:

a There are lots of things for children to do in Eastlands, therefore you will never be bored here.

b Eastlands is close to the city; however, the parks make it feel as if it's in the country.

**Step 3**

1 **b**

2 Suggested answer: Now that you know what a great place Eastlands is, I am sure you will want to live here. I can't wait for you to move here.

## Page 47

Dear Paula and Tessa

I am so excited you are moving to Melbourne! When you get here, I believe you should live in Eastlands. I am sure you will want to when I tell you what a great place it is.

Firstly, you can buy anything you need in Eastlands, from food to furniture. There is a large supermarket and hardware store, as well as many other interesting shops. But that's just one of the reasons I like living here.

Secondly, Eastlands has an excellent public transport system, so it is easy to get to and from the city. We have a regular bus service and there is a train station in the middle of the suburb. Also, the trains and buses are always on time!

Finally, there are lots of places in Eastlands where you can relax and have fun. It has two beautiful parks and lots of cafes and restaurants. There is also a great skateboard park and a large public swimming pool, so there is plenty for children to do. In addition, it is close to the beach!

Now that you know what a great place Eastlands is, I am sure you will want to live here. I really enjoy living here, and I can't wait for you to move here. We are going to have so much fun!

Love, Sienna

# Unit 5 Writing a narrative

## Page 49

1 **a** two little polar bears **b** on an iceberg **c** explore an iceberg

2 The iceberg started drifting out to sea.

3 They screamed.

4 Their mother rescued them.

## Page 50

1 They were terrified. 2 They felt silly.

## Page 51

1 **a, b, c, e, g, h**

2 **a** had **b** saw **c** told **d** said **e** felt

3 It's an animal that lives mainly in the water and looks like an alligator.

## Pages 52–53

**Step 1**

1 twittering 2 swishing 3 trailing 4 peeping

**Step 2**

1 saucers 2 leaf 3 jelly 4 sheet 5 butterfly

**Step 3**

1 **b** 2 **a**

3 **a** Tom shouted, "Meg! Get your hand out of the water!"

**b** "Why?" she asked.

**c** "A c-c-crocodile," stuttered Tom. "Over there!"

**d** "Don't worry, Meg," said Tom, "I won't let it get us."

4 **a** Tom said, "I really thought that was a crocodile."

**b** "Oh, Tom," said Meg, "you gave me such a fright."

**c** "Let's not tell anyone how silly we were," said Tom.

## Page 54

1 in the woods, the stream

2 was trailing, twittering, swishing

3 "Meg! Get your hand out of the water!"

4 as big as saucers

5 Quickly

## Page 55

1 Humpty got the idea to climb up the wall when he saw a ladder in the shed.

2 Luckily, the doctor was able to put Humpty's head back together.

## Page 56

1 **a, b, c, d, e, g**

2 **a** curious **b** dusty **c** great stone

3 to show that the men belonged to the king

## Pages 57–58

**Step 1**

1 noticed 2 dragged 3 clambered 4 peer 5 wobble 6 tumbling 7 raced

**Step 2**

1 **a** 2 **b**

2 **a** "Will he be all right?" asked Gumpty and Lumpty.

**b** The doctor replied, "He's going to be just fine!"

**Step 3**

Suggested answer: Carefully, they lifted him onto a horse and rushed him to hospital. Luckily, the doctor was able to stitch Humpty's head back together, and soon he was as good as new!

## Page 59

**Humpty's great fall**

One morning Humpty was playing hide-and-seek with his brothers and sisters in the palace gardens. Of all the king's children, Humpty was the most curious.

While he was hiding inside a dusty shed, he noticed a ladder in the corner. It gave him an idea.

Later that morning, Humpty asked his brothers, Gumpty and Lumpty, to help him carry the ladder to the great stone wall.

"What are you going to do with it?" asked Gumpty.

"I'm going to climb to the top of the wall to see what's on the other side," announced Humpty.

The three little princes dragged the ladder to the wall. Gumpty and Lumpty held it steady while Humpty clambered to the top. He was just about to peer over the wall when the ladder started to wobble. Humpty lost his balance and came tumbling down. He hit the ground with a loud thud.

"Help! Help!" cried Gumpty and Lumpty. "Humpty's had a terrible accident!"

The king's men raced to help the little prince. They found him with his head cracked open!

Carefully, they lifted him onto a horse and rushed him to hospital. Luckily, the doctor was able to stitch Humpty's head back together, and soon he was as good as new!

# Unit 6 Writing an information report

## Page 61

1 a and d    2 b, d and e

## Page 62

1 Apples are good for us because they contain vitamins and minerals.

2 Apples are grown in all Australian states.

## Page 63

1 c, e, f, g, h    2 a round    b green, red

## Pages 64–65

**Step 1**

Suggested answer: An apple is an edible fruit. That means we can eat it. Apples are part of the rose family.

**Step 2**

Suggested answers:

1 … green, yellow, pink, orange-red or dark red.

2 … Granny Smith, Red Delicious, Pink Lady, Fuji, Gala and Golden Delicious.

3 … New South Wales, Victoria and Tasmania.

4 … they are grown throughout the world.

**Step 3**

1 b, c, f

2 Apples are my favourite fruit.
I think everyone should eat more apples.

3 Suggested answer: A watermelon has a thick skin.

4 a, b and d are the facts.

## Page 66

1 edible    2 round

3 Granny Smith, Red Delicious, Pink Lady, Golden Delicious, Gala, Fuji

4 The apples are picked in the autumn.

5 New South Wales, Victoria, Tasmania

6 all around the world

## Page 67

1 long, curved    2 bunch

## Page 68

1 b, c, f, g, h

2 I think bananas are the best kind of fruit.
I think they are the healthiest snack.

## Pages 69–70

**Step 1**

A banana is an edible fruit. It is part of the lily and orchid family.

**Step 2**

1 Cavendish, Lady Finger

2 a hand    b finger

3 Suggested answer: Bananas are healthy because they contain carbohydrates, vitamins and minerals.

**Step 3**

1 trees, bunches

2 … the bunches are very heavy … in storage compartments at the markets.

**Step 4**

1 F    2 O    3 O    4 F    5 O    6 F

## Page 71

**Bananas**

**Introduction**

A banana is an edible fruit. It is part of the lily and orchid family.

**Appearance**

A banana is a long, curved fruit. It has a thick, yellow skin and soft, creamy white flesh. Bananas are between 15 and 25 cm long.

**Varieties**

There are two main varieties of banana, the Cavendish and the Lady Finger. The Cavendish is about 20 to 25 cm long. The Lady Finger is only about 15 cm long, but is fatter than the Cavendish.

**How bananas grow**

Bananas grow in bunches on tall plants that look like trees. One layer of bananas in a bunch is called a hand, and a single banana is called a finger.

**Where bananas are grown**

In Australia, bananas are grown mainly in Queensland, northern New South Wales, the Northern Territory and Western Australia.

**When bananas are grown**

Bananas are grown all year round in Australia.

**Nutritional value**

Bananas are healthy to eat because they contain carbohydrates, vitamins and minerals.

**Interesting facts**

Bananas are picked by hand when they are still green. This is because they go rotten very quickly once they ripen. The green bunches are sent to the markets, where they are ripened in special compartments.

Because the bunches are so heavy, two people are needed to harvest a single bunch.

## Unit 7 Writing to give advice—holiday reviews

### Page 73

A

### Page 74

1 Kakadu National Park, Northern Territory, Darwin, Warradjan Aboriginal Cultural Centre, Yellow Waters Wetland
2 Bininj
3 Suggestion: The photo shows Aboriginal rock art.

### Page 75

1 b, d
2 a present b future c past
3 wild horse

### Pages 76–77

**Step 1**

July, the Northern Territory, 171 km south-east of Darwin.

**Step 2**

Suggested answer: One of the things you can do in Kakadu is go to the Warradjan Aboriginal Cultural Centre. Warradjan is an Aboriginal name that means pig-nosed turtle. The building is round, just like a turtle. It has lots of interesting information about Aboriginal culture.

**Step 3**

1 a wonderful b adventurous c interesting d exciting e good
2 a waterfall b lake c lilies d eagle
3 Suggested answer: Watching the whales was an amazing experience.

### Page 78

1 The park is in the Northern Territory, about 171 km south-east of Darwin.
2 interesting 3 good 4 huge
5 Just take lots of insect repellent to keep the flies and mosquitoes away!

### Page 79

1 The ground in the caves could be uneven and slippery, so visitors would need sturdy shoes.
2 It could be cool inside the caves, so visitors would need jumpers or jackets.
3 stalagmites

### Page 80

1 b, d
2 a are, is used b went, couldn't, took, wore
3 a huge b sturdy c cool

### Pages 81–82

**Step 1**

The Jenolan Caves are in the Blue Mountains World Heritage area in New South Wales. They are about 180 km west of Sydney.

**Step 2**

The caves are millions of years old. The bones of Ice Age animals are buried deep inside them.

**Step 3**

1 a amazing b magnificent/magical c magnificent/magical
2 a arch/rock formations b path/rocks c lake/plants d buildings
3 Suggested answer: The views in the Blue Mountains are spectacular.

### Page 83

**The Jenolan Caves**

I visited the Jenolan Caves with my family in the school holidays. These amazing caves are in the Blue Mountains World Heritage area in New South Wales. They are about 180 km west of Sydney.

There are ten caves that are open to the public, so we couldn't see them all. We took the tour through the Lucas, Imperial and Chifley Caves. The stalactites and stalagmites in the caves are a magnificent sight.

Our guide was very friendly and helpful. She knew a lot about the caves. She told us that they are millions of years old and that the bones of Ice Age animals are buried deep inside them.

The Lucas Cave has the largest chambers. The biggest chamber, The Cathedral, is 54 m high. It is often used for musical performances because of its brilliant acoustics.

Visiting the Jenolan Caves is a magical experience. If you live in Sydney, you can easily go there for the day. Just remember to wear old clothes, sturdy shoes and to take a pullover or jacket with you. It is always cool inside the caves.

# Unit 8 Explaining how a simple machine works

## Page 85

1 present  2 First, Then  3 magnifies
4 telescope, lens, eyepiece

## Page 86

1

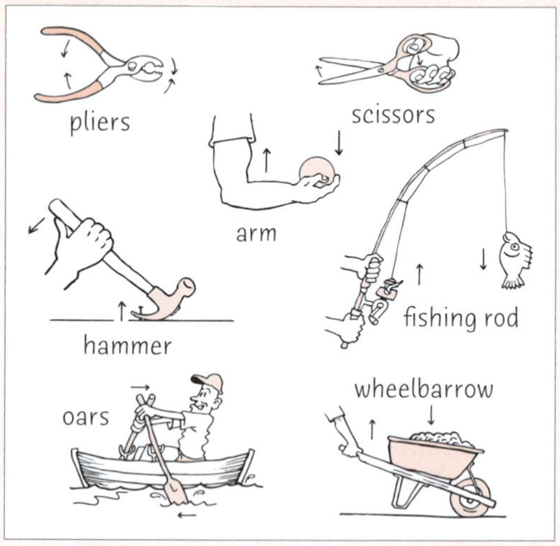


2 oars

3 a hammer  b oars  c arm
d fishing rod

## Page 87

1 a, b, e  2 pushed, moved

## Pages 88–89

### Step 1

2

### Step 2

1 fulcrum  2 force  3 load

### Step 3

1 turns  2 is, works  3 applies
4 moves  5 are

### Step 4

People have been using levers for centuries. They are very useful machines, especially when they are combined with other simple machines like wedges and wheels.

## Page 90

1 makes work easier
2 scissors, staplers, pliers and wheelbarrows
3 fulcrum  4 First, then  5 for centuries

## Page 91

1 a bicycle and a flagpole

2

3 ... pushing down on the pedals.

## Page 92

1 a, b, d  2 was, went, pulled, moved
3 a lower  b tied  c pulled

## Pages 93–94

### Step 1

A pulley is a simple machine that makes it easier to lift and lower things.

### Step 2

1 build, lift, make, use, work, fasten, start, raise
2 a are  b is  c pulls
d moves  e have  f can

### Step 3

Suggested answer: Some very big pulleys, like cranes, have more than one wheel. They use steel cables instead of ropes. These big pulleys can move very heavy loads.

## Page 95

A pulley is a simple machine that uses a wheel and a rope to lift, lower or move a load.

A flagpole is a good example of a simple pulley. A rope, which is twice as long as the pole, is passed through a wheel at the top of the flagpole. The flag is then attached to one end of the rope. Finally, someone pulls on the other end of the rope and the flag moves up the pole.

Some very big pulleys, like cranes, have more than one wheel. They use steel cables instead of ropes. These big pulleys can move very heavy loads.

# Word bank

## Unit 1 Writing a recount

### Time connectives to link ideas:

| | | | |
|---|---|---|---|
| after that | afterwards | before | first |
| first of all | finally | last of all | lastly |
| next | then | | |

### Phrases that tell how, where and when:

**How:** These phrases mainly start with words like *with, in* and *by*.

They handled it **with great care**.

He did it **in a hurry**.

They sat **in silence**.

We travelled **by bus**.

**Where:** These phrases mainly start with words like *across, around, at, beside, by, in, on, over, through* and *under*.

We drove **across the bridge**.

He ran **around the track**.

I will see you **at school**.

She sat **beside her friend**.

He is standing **by the lake**.

Put your socks **in the drawer**.

Your keys are **on the table**.

He kicked the ball **over the fence**.

He looked **through the window**.

His bag is **under the table**.

**When:** These phrases mainly start with words like *after, at, before, during, in* and *on*.

I met him **after lunch**.

They arrived **at six o'clock**.

Finish it **before next week**.

I coughed a lot **during the night**.

I will be there **in an hour**.

We got there **on time**.

## Unit 2 Writing a procedure

### Action verbs that might be useful in procedures:

| | | | | |
|---|---|---|---|---|
| add | chop | close | colour | cut |
| decorate | fold | glue | measure | mix |
| open | place | press | put | serve |
| slice | stir | tape | trim | wash |

## Unit 3 Describing a person

### Adjectives that describe a person's appearance:

**Eyes:** bright, twinkling

**Hair:** blonde (female) blond (male), curly, dark, fair, golden, straight, wavy

**Height:** medium, short, tall

**Size:** chubby, enormous, gigantic, huge, muscular, plump, skinny, slim, strong, tiny, well-built

**Skin:** pale, rough, smooth, wrinkled

**General:** attractive, beautiful, clumsy, handsome, hideous, lovely, pretty

**Qualities:**

adventurous, brave, courageous, determined

calm, patient, quiet

clever, intelligent, smart

curious, inquisitive

energetic, healthy, lively

friendly, helpful, kind, polite

funny, amusing

gentle, loving

honest, responsible, sensible, trustworthy

stylish, fashionable

unselfish, generous

## Unit 4 Writing to persuade—expositions

### Connectives to link ideas:

| | | | |
|---|---|---|---|
| after that | finally | first | firstly |
| lastly | next | secondly | then |

## Unit 5 Writing a narrative

### Adjectives that describe how people and things sound:

deafening, faint, muffled, noisy, quiet, rowdy

### Adjectives that describe how people and things feel:

boiling, bumpy, cold, cool, damp, freezing, hard, hot, rough, silky, soft, soggy, warm, wet

**Adjectives that describe how people and things smell:**

disgusting, sweet

**Adjectives that describe how people and things taste:**

creamy, crisp, crunchy, delicious, hot, scrumptious, spicy, sweet, tasty

**Descriptive verbs:**

ask, beg

climb, clamber, scramble

eat, munch

fall, slip, tumble

fly, float, glide, swoop

hold, clutch, grab

laugh, chuckle, giggle

look (at), gaze, stare

pull, tug

push, shove

run, dash, sprint

say, announce, remark

see, spot

shake, shiver, tremble

shout, scream, yell

sigh, gasp, pant

sleep, doze, snooze

walk, stroll, stride

**Common similes:**

| | |
|---|---|
| as busy as a bee | to flutter like a butterfly |
| as delicate as a flower | to gleam like a pearl |
| as fit as a fiddle | to have eyes like a hawk |
| as free as a bird | to run like the wind |
| as gentle as a lamb | to shake like a leaf |
| as quick as a wink | to sleep like a baby |
| as slippery as an eel | to sing like an angel |
| eyes as big as saucers | to sparkle like a diamond |

## Unit 6 Writing an information report

**Technical language:**

This will depend on the subject you are writing about. For example:

**Birds** beak, crest, plumage

**Computers** keyboard, monitor, mouse

**Countries** continent, island, population

**Plants** germinate, pollinate, seedling

**Storms** blizzard, cyclone, hurricane

## Unit 7 Writing to give advice—holiday reviews

**Adjectives that show opinions:**

amazing, brilliant, fantastic

boring, dull

difficult, hard, challenging

easy, simple

exciting, adventurous

funny, amusing

good, excellent, great

interesting, fascinating

magical, magnificent, spectacular

strange, odd, weird

unusual, unexpected

## Unit 8 Explaining how a simple machine works

**Technical language:**

This will depend on the subject you are writing about. For example:

**Axe** handle, steel, wedge

**Bicycle** axle, chain, pedal, saddle, wheel

**Tap** pipe, screw, washer

**Windmill** blade, tower, turbine

**Yacht** hull, keel, mast, rudder, sail